The Little Book of MAGICAL WEDDING Ideas

Your Magic Wand to help you plan your wedding

The Little Book of MAGICAL WEDDING Ideas

Hundreds of **BIG CREATIVE IDEAS** for any wedding!

Magic Wand Publishing
www. magicwandweddings.com
e-mail: info@magicwandweddings.com

ISBN: 0-9711909-0-9

Spirit of Romance

Empowerment of Creativity

Magic of Happily Ever After

Author

Once upon a time when I was a little girl, my best friend and I used to plan pretend weddings together. We always dreamed of organizing real ceremonies right down to the last detail. As flower girls at family weddings, we would compare notes and make pretend changes. As I grew older, I continued to inquire into and make notes concerning every detail of every wedding I organized, attended, or was mentioned to me. These notes helped me plan and execute my own fairy-tale marriage, which took place in the romantic highlands of Scotland. It was a truly wonderful experience, and included a kilt, castle, and bagpipes. Now, as a wedding consultant, I would like to share the Little Book of Magical Wedding Ideas with you. It's a fun, easy-to-use, and magical source of inspiration that will help you create a lifetime of beautiful wedding memories.

Lisa Hughes

Member of the Association of Bridal Consultants

Acknowledgements

The Little Book of Magical Wedding Ideas is based on extensive research, first-hand interviews, and my own experiences. I'd like to thank the many couples I interviewed for their willingness to share with me the special moments of their engagements and weddings, and for allowing me to share them with others. Their ideas and memories served as the inspiration for this book. Special thanks to my editors, Pat Hughes, Sarah Lawrence, and Sharon Rice. Thanks also to, Marcia, Ariel, and Bradley, for their inspiration, and to my cat Sushi who served as my writing companion during the wee hours of the night.

Author and back cover photo courtesy of
Kenny Ferguson Photography, Fort William, Scotland.
www.kennyfergusonphotography.co.uk.com

Preface

Weddings are a wonderful and public declaration of two people's commitment to one another and a fantastic celebration of their love. Weddings represent society's hopes and dreams for the future, and they strengthen the fabric of our society. Weddings represent joyous times in our lives ...so let the wedding bells ring.

This book is dedicated to all the future brides.

Engagement Announcements

invitations

Ceremony Ideas

Reception Ideas

Table of Contents

Introduction

Congratulations! If you're reading this book, you've probably begun to plan your wedding day. You're probably looking for new ideas to customize every aspect of the big event and achieve just the right look and feel. Planning even a small wedding takes quite a bit of preparation. Planning a medium to large wedding is even more involved. To put it in perspective, it's as though you're the conductor of an orchestra preparing for opening night. You must book an auditorium, hire the backstage crew, write the music, plan the musical sequences, and then conduct and perform live on stage before an audience. For most of us that seems like a daunting task especially if you're on a tight budget, however, it's much easier if you have the right planning tools. *The Little Book of MAGICAL WEDDING Ideas* was written specifically to address the needs of brides-to-be who are looking not just for creative inspiration, but practical tips. So, are you ready to begin? Then let's set the stage, cue the lights, and get started.

MAGICAL

Engagement Announcements

Wow, congratulations on your engagement! Now, lets start spreading the news. First, you must decide who you'd like to include in your announcement list, and then what kind of announcement they'll receive. For example, you may wish to give your coworkers a less formal announcement than you give to your close friends or family members. Then, you must consider whether you want to take a humorous or lighthearted approach to the design of your announcement, or one that's serious or dramatic. Not sure where to begin? In this section you'll find a range of fun, creative, and romantic ways to announce your big news, so relax, have fun, and be creative.

Get a Wedding Website

Create and upload your personal wedding website, beginning with the engagement announcement, with up-to-date details, photos and anecdotes for friends and family.

Electronic Newsletter

Send guests a wedding electronic newsletter. Include information about the big day as well as travel information of the area hotels and restaurants. Many word processing programs have easy to use templates.

Vacation Time

Put in your vacation request from work as early as possible.

Family and Friends Gathering

Have a gathering of friends and family, and to tell anyone of the announcement. It can be either formal or casual and can be as large or as small as you wish.

Get the Word Out

Print and mail the announcement, or fax and e-mail the announcement to friends and family. Don't leave anyone out who might be offended by not receiving the good news.

Coming Soon

Send your engagement announcement as an advertisement for a new upcoming movie. "Coming Soon to a Chapel Near You", starring... (Couples name). Include a photo of couple and brief description of the event (movie).

Hire an Actor
Hire an actor to announce your engagement to all by reciting lines from well-known plays and movies and relating them to relevant anecdotes of the couple.

Beach Party in the Sky
Have a beach party and hire a sky writer to announce your engagement. Make it a big public declaration.

PBS Announcement
Become a member of PBS during a televised fundraiser and donate (in yours and your new fiancés name) a small donation with your engagement announcement on TV. Make sure you videotape the announcement.

Holiday Time
If your engagement comes around the holiday season, include your engagement details in your holiday cards. Include an engagement photo if you wish.

Send a Video Announcement
Make a movie for your friends and family giving them the details on a video.

Electronic Greeting Cards
Send out an electronic greeting card announcing the great news. You can find them on the Internet at bluemountain.com or from similar websites. Best of all…it's free.

Up in the Sky
At an outside event, have a plane with banner announce your engagement and videotape the plane to show later.

Tell Your Office
To get the word out to your boss and co-workers, bring in a cake and sparkling cider on a Friday afternoon to announce the news. Everybody loves food. Now 's the time to ask for that vacation time for your honeymoon.

Literally Tie the Knot

Go to a fine paper store and purchase some nice paper, envelopes and thin ribbon. Print out on your desktop printer the message "Guess Who's Going To Tie The Knot" and include your names and information. Then at the top of the paper, punch two small holes with a hole-punch in the top center and tie the ribbon into a knot. This is simple, fun and affordable.

Paid Advertising

Take out your very own display ad in your local newspaper. Most newspapers have an art department on site that can put the ads together for you. For people who don't live in your area, photocopy and mail them the ad.

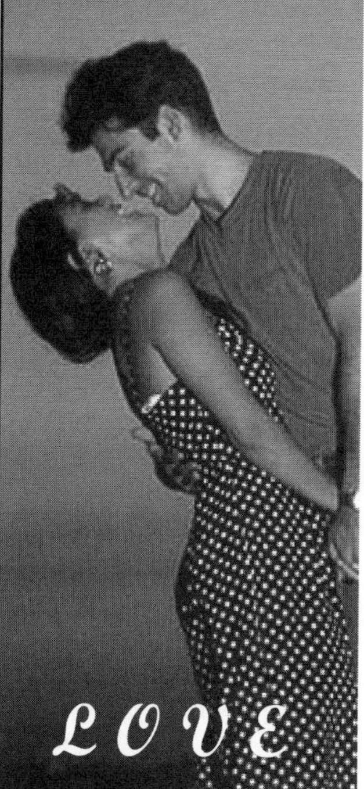

I Asked.

She said "YES".

We Will.

June 2002.

Chris Smith &
Donna Jones
(future husband and wife)

Start a Wedding Journal

Start keeping a wedding journal now, you'll be happy you did. Especially when you look back and reflect on one of the best times of your life. Include everything from the proposal to the last minute of your honemoon.

Plan a Gathering with Friends and Family

If serving beer, include on the beer bottles, labels saying "Beers to yous, here's the news - guess who's engaged" and include your names and information. Use desktop printing labels that will easily fit into your desktop printer. Be creative and have lots of fun. Have a special toast with your engagement beer bottles. Your guests will want them as mementos.

***"Special of the Day"* Announcement**

Plan to go to dinner at your favorite restaurant with family and close friends. Ahead of time, make up a pretend flyer menu of the special of the day and give to your server to pass out with the regular menus. "Wedding Announcement Plate Special", prepared exclusively for close friends and family from the newly engaged couple of… Print from your desktop printer.

Menu

Special of the Day

Appetizer: **Glass of Champagne**

Entree: **The Engagement of Richard & Monica**

Dessert: **April 20th**

We wish to thank

everyone

for their love and support

Junk Mail Announcement

If you choose to send your announcements by mail, here's a fun way! Simply print out from your desktop printer something that looks like junk mail and hand deliver or mail. Include your pictures and engagement information on the outside. Make a 3-fold letter style and close it with a staple or round label. Make sure on the outside that it includes your names, very large, and special attention required in bold.

Keep the Announcement a Surprise

Plan a gathering with friends and family at a public sports event, baseball, basketball, hockey, football, etc. Coordinate ahead of time with the announcer to announce your new fiancé (her name) is waiting for you at the main entrance. Better yet, request an announcement over the loudspeaker of your engagement and have their cameras put you up on the big screen.

punch hole punch hole

SEASON TICKET ANNOUNCEMENT

Tango Style

For something special, create your announcements with some flair. Strike a dance position (tango style) with a big smile. Word the headline on the outside or at the top, "*Two to Tango... It's a lifelong dance*". Frame the photograph as a creative reminder of the special occasion. You could add a top hat and tails for more fun.

Announcing the Dance for the Rest of Our Lives!

Paula & Jim

Engaged May 25th

Here Ye Here Ye Announcement

If you have a theatrical flair, complete your Renaissance theme with announcements that fit the part.

Send a Paper Airplane Announcement "AirMail"

Fold a paper airplane and follow the lines and draw them as guides in your word processing program. This will tell your recipients how to fold your aerodynamic announcement. It is a fun and creative way to announce the big news. You can easily create this on your desktop.

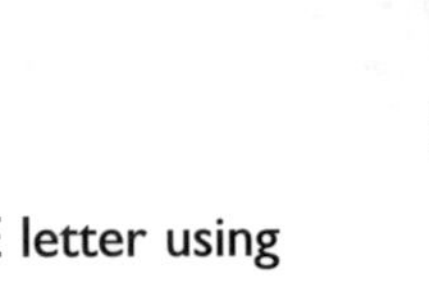

L O V E letter. Create a real L O V E letter using slightly elevated letters above the type.

Love's not time's fool, though rosy lips and cheeks

Within his bending sickle's c**O**mpass come,

Love alters not with his brief hours and weeks,

But bears it out e**V**en to the edge of doom:

If this be error, and upon me proved,

I never writ, nor no man ever lov**e**d.

–Sonnet 116, William Shakespeare

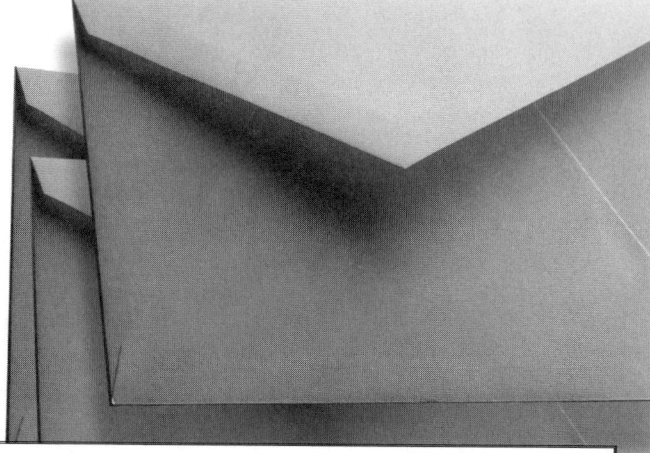

Let me not to the marriage of true minds
Admit impediments. Love is not love
Which alters when it alteration finds
Or bends with the remover to remove.
O, no, it is an ever fixed mark
That looks on tempests and is never shaken,
It is the star to every wandering bark,
Whose worth's unknown, although his height be taken.
Love's not time's fool, though rosy lips and cheeks
Within his bending sickle's compass come,
Love alters not with his brief hours and weeks,
But bears it out even to the edge of doom:
If this be error, and upon me proved,
I never writ, nor no man ever loved.
--Sonnet 116, William Shakespeare

USHERS

Maid of Honor

Bridesmaids

Ring Bearer

BEST MAN

Flower Girl

MAGICAL

Wedding Party

The wedding party… the words even sound fun! It should be great fun and memory filled. Remember, you're the orchestra conductor, so select individuals for your wedding party who complement your personality and who will fit in well with the other members of the wedding party. Task your wedding party to assist you with assignments such as decorating, choosing a caterer, food and music selection, reviewing possible locations, making centerpieces, coordinating special events, ushering guests, etc. As conductor, you also determine your wedding's theme through the selection of colors and types of clothing, and the introduction of ethnic and religious influences. Want a Scottish theme? Consider having the men of the wedding party wear kilts. Instead of a black tie affair, why not a red and black affair? Ask the men to wear a red cummerbund and red socks. Wish to include or pay tribute to another culture in your wedding theme? Have your wedding party wear traditional clothing or include only an accent, such as a hat or scarf. Ask the more inventive or extroverted members of your wedding party to entertain your guests with a fun, two-minute song and dance routine. You're in charge, so enjoy yourself and maintain a good attitude through the big event.

Need Some Help with the Planning?
Put a list of tasks in a hat on single strips of paper and ask your bridesmaids to draw from the hat to find out what their responsibilities will be. They can trade afterwards if they wish and this will leave you impartial.

Special Pre-Wedding Thanks
Invite the wedding party out and uncork some pre-wedding champagne and take a moment to thank everyone in the wedding and give some toasts. Then get down to business and discuss the day in detail, time to be at the place of worship, wedding rings, etc. Put together a schedule of events for the day to pass out to everyone so the wedding party will all be on the same page. It seems more fun and magical if it's presented as such in the beginning and people are more willing to help rather than feel it's an obligation.

Male of Honor
How about having a "Male of Honor"? Is your closest friend the opposite sex? Go ahead and have a male "maid of honor" or bridesmaid.

What About Different Colors?
When selecting bridesmaid dresses, try selecting different styles and even colors that look nice together.

Let the Bridesmaids Decide
Instead of selecting the bridesmaid's dresses, try sending them swatches of your wedding colors and let them go and select their own dress. What a magical surprise to see what everyone selects.

Magical Maid of Honor
To distinguish the maid of honor from the others, make their bouquet larger or put them in a different color.

Lights, Camera, Action
Make a magical movie speech. For the Best Man who wants to do something different for that big speech, how about producing a short video. Include footage of the bride and groom and do interviews with family and friends to make the video more fun. Add music if possible. You can find many computer software programs that can help do this for you.

Staying Warm at Winter Weddings
If you're having a winter wedding, give a warm gift. A warm and soft Pashmina shawl to wear in the wedding over cold shoulders. This becomes a special article of significant clothing and could be handed down to the children. www.cashmerecompany.com

Rehearsal Time

At your rehearsal dinner, buy a variety of gifts, one for each attendant. Put all of their names in a hat, and have the bride and groom pull names to see who gets what. They can always exchange afterwards.

Entertaining Wedding Party

As entertainment at the reception, have your wedding party bring their sunglasses and lip sync and perform a very simple dance routine to one of their favorite songs dedicated to the bride and groom. A magical moment you'll never forget.

Baby Pictures

At the rehearsal dinner, frame a baby picture of the bride and groom and as an option, include one of their wedding invitations in the center. This is something they will keep forever as a magical memento.

In Honor of Remembering

Have the wedding party wear a simple colored ribbon on the men's lapel or pinned on the women's dress or hair, in honor of someone who was not able to attend (living or not), or towards a special cause or belief.

Color Themes

After you've determined your theme colors, such as red, white, pink, purple, etc., purchase the same color coordinated socks for each of the men in the wedding party to wear in solidarity. If only one man wears the sock color, it's considered rebellious. But, if they all wear them, it's considered fashionable.

Fun Summer Wedding

Ask your ushers and best man to dress in their favorite swimming trunks and flip flops with the traditional tuxedo jacket and tie.

The Fred Astaire Look

Have all the men in the wedding party wear top hats, white gloves, carry canes and tuxedos with tails. Classically magical.

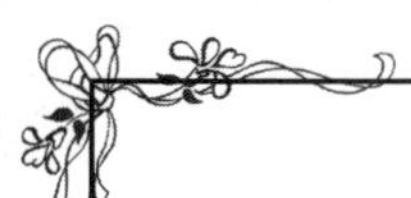

Thank You Gift Ideas

To thank your wedding party for all their hard work here's a few suggestions for gifts: 2 movie passes with popcorn and sodas included, Magazine subscriptions, Gift certificate from their favorite restaurant, A day at a spa, Subscription to Harry and David "Fruit of the Month Club", SmithHawkin flowers of the month delivered, On-line gift certificate to Amazon.com for books and music, or Starbucks gift certificate. Let your creativity go wild.

Flower Child

Dress your little flower girl in shiney Mary Jane shoes and a halo of fresh flowers in her hair with a big satin ribbon trailing down the back.

Handmade Paper

BLESSED BY THE POPE

LOVE LETTERS

Message in a Bottle

Invitations & Announcements

The big day is approaching and it's time to send out invitations to your friends and loved ones. What will they look like? What will they say? In their simplest form, wedding invitations are vehicles for sharing information, but invest a little thought into their design and they can also provide your guests with a glimpse of the magic to come. Are you planning a contemporary wedding? One that's playful or sophisticated or a fairytale come true? Through the design of your invitation, you can begin to stimulate interest in your wedding well in advance of the actual event. Not sure how or where to begin? Here are a few suggestions to free your imagination and help you conjure up your own magical wedding invitation ideas.

Be Creative

Try designing your own invitations and announcements. Many fine stationary stores carry handmade paper and beautiful preprinted stationary to make your invitations look professional and are tailored to your needs. Simply write your wording and print on your own printer.

Fairytale Feel

Try using parchment paper accompanied by beautiful calligraphy lettering to give a fairytale feel. Add a little glitter into each invitation to sprinkle out when opened for a magical effect.

Message in a Bottle

Use sealing wax and stamp the initial of your new last name at the top of the invitation. Roll up the invitations using satin ribbon to tie them and keep them from uncurling. Don't forget to include the reply notes and envelopes. Place in a tube. You can find tubes at your local shipping/mailing office products store. This will give your invitations a special regal European look.

Start Spreading the News

Send announcements to local newspapers, place of worship, your high school and college alumni including a special story of how you met.

Handmade Paper

Handmade papers with flowers pressed into the paper for a romantic look, include a little potpourri inside each invitation.

Red Heart Confetti

Sprinkle little red heart confetti inside each invitation for Valentine's Day theme weddings.

Shaped Invitations

Be different and select shaped invitations such as the bride and groom, hearts, glass slippers, martini glasses, champagne bottles etc.

Traditional look

Use engraved invitations on pure white or ivory paper printed in script. For the very untraditional, use black paper and white or silver ink with accents of red or a picture of a rose.

Floral Scented

Spray a floral scented perfume onto the invitations. Use a script or curly typestyle. Make your own invitations and glue a flat dried flower at the top or bottom. Include a famous French wedding phrase at the top or bottom (check internet for verbage).

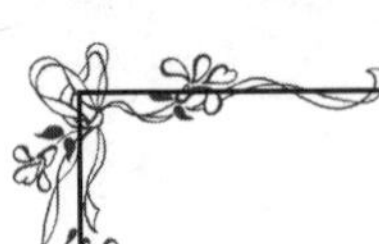

Medieval Look
Give your invitation a real European medieval look and seal the envelopes with sealing wax stamped with your new last name initial and small swatch of cut ribbon.

Stay Organized
Create a spreadsheet with everyone you've invited including names, addresses and phone numbers. This will make life easier when it's time to write thank you notes.

Favorite Songs
On the reception reply cards sent with your invitations, ask your guests to include five of their favorite songs. Give your DJ all the requests and everyone will hear at least one of their favorite songs.

Just In Case

Keep a few extra invitations ready to go, for any overlooked guests.

Calligraphy Styles

Calligraphy is a beautiful touch to any invitation, announcement and addressed envelopes. Today's costs for hand writing calligraphy can get quite expensive. You may decide to use a computer typeface that will give the same effect that is more cost effective on all of those envelopes to be addressed. Here are a few samples of typefaces that have the calligraphy look and are easily read;

Mr. and Mrs. Mark Spencer

Mr. and Mrs. Mark Spencer

Mr. and Mrs. Mark Spencer

Mr. and Mrs. Mark Spencer

Mr. and Mrs. Mark Spencer

Mr. and Mrs. Mark Spencer

MR. AND MRS. MARK SPENCER

Mr. and Mrs. Mark Spencer

Mr. and Mrs. Mark Spencer

Mr. and Mrs. Mark Spencer

Mr. and Mrs. Mark Spencer

Mr and Mrs Mark Spencer

Mr. and Mrs. Mark Spencer

Mr. and Mrs. Mark Spencer

Mr. and Mrs. Mark Spencer

MR. AND MRS. MARK SPENCER

Mr. and Mrs. Mark Spencer

Mr. and Mrs. Mark Spencer

Invitations

If you travel to Rome, you could arrange to see the Pope at a service. Get more information from your local priest.

Blessed by the Pope

Make it a regal experience and have your invitations memorialized by the Vatican. It's possible to have your wedding invitations blessed by the Pope, however you must be Catholic for the blessing. Send your wedding invitation with a donation to the Vatican and you'll receive a document worth framing for a lifelong memento. Inquire with your local priest for more details.

Computer and Software

Art Classes

Honeymoon Fund

American Express Gift Checques

Gourmet Cooking Classes

Maid Service

MAGICAL

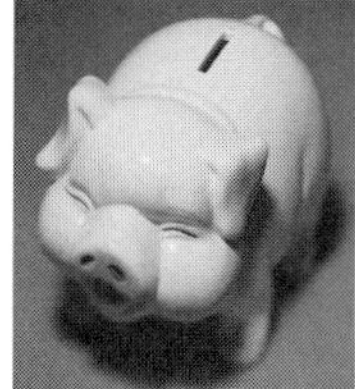

Gift Registry

Today's gift registry is no longer limited to a national department store or to household gift items, but rather it's tailored to the couple's interests and desires. Be creative with your registry and get what you and your fiancé really want and need.

Invitation Spreadsheet

When you start to receive gifts, enter the gift to your invitation spreadsheet. This will keep everything in one place and thank you notes will be much simpler.

Guests Will Find Out

Do not include where you are registered on your wedding invitations. Guests will ask and find out.

Proper Etiquette

Today's proper etiquette says it is okay to include registry information on wedding shower invitations.

Register with a Travel Agency

You are able to set up a trip registry at your local travel agency. Your guests will be able to help with the honeymoon fund.

How About Luggage?

You can always use new luggage especially on your honeymoon.

Gift Budgets

Remember everyone's budget for gifts is different. Include all price ranges from small kitchen items to large ticket items such as a television.

Cigar Lover's Magazine

Cigar Aficionado www.cigaraficionado.com

The Official New Bride Name Change Kit
www.kitbiz.com is a complete name change kit for the bride to help make life easier when it's time to do name change information.

National Standard Department Stores
Macy's, Robinson's/May, Sears, JC Penney's, etc. are always a great selection.

Gourmet Cooking
William Sonoma is a perfect registry to have for the gourmet cooks. It's a gourmet heaven for home chefs.

Creative Home Furnishings
Crate & Barrel and Pottery Barn for contemporary home furnishings.

Giftcertificates.com
Gift certificates for 700 stores, airlines, restaurants, hotels and more. Gift certificates can even be e-mailed to recipients.

Candles Everywhere
Illuminations.com, beautiful candles to use for the wedding or reception or for your new home together.

Museumshop.com
Gifts from 40 of the world's finest museums.

Sharperimage.com
Get the latest high tech gadgets.

Home Depot Gift Certificates
For the do-it-yourself couple's new house or apartment.

Gourmet Pots & Pans
After a cooking class in Tuscany, you're sure to want some professional pots and pans, like a real chef.

American Express Gift Cheques

Put an American Express Gift Cheque toward anything you can imagine such as:

A new computer

Towards a new car

Specialty gourmet cooking classes

Museum memberships to your favorite museum

Tickets for Ski-lifts at your favorite resort

Dance lessons

Art classes

A local weekend getaway

Maid service for the first 6 months

A day at the spa

Artwork to decorate your new home

Plants and flowers for your new home

Two round trip tickets to anywhere

A new puppy

Toward a down-payment for a house or apartment

Honeymoon spending money

On-Line Registries

Tiffany & Co.	www.tiffany.com
Crate & Barrel	www.crateandbarrel.com
Williams Sonoma	www.williams-sonoma.com
Restoration Hardware	www.restorationhardware.com
REI	www.rei.com
Bloomingdales	www.bloomingdales.com
Macy's	www.macys.com
Gumps	www.gumps.com
Dean & Deluca	www.deandeluca.com
Ross Simons	www.ross-simons.com
Pottery Barn	www.potterybarn.com
Smith Hawkin	www.smithhawkin.com

CookingClasses

COMPUTERS

Music Lessons

Universal Studios Movie Set

ON A ROOF TOP IN L.A.

Empire State Building

BOND 007 PUB

Disneyland

Locations

Location, location, location. The location you choose will serve as the stage for your exchange of vows and wedding celebration, so it is very important that it reflect both you and your fiancé's interests. Consider what aspects of a location will make it memorable for you and your guests? Will it harmonize with the theme of your wedding? Does it involve travel? Must it take place in a foreign locale or is there an alternative setting closer to home? Let the following ideas spark your enthusiasm, and perhaps take you in a direction you've never before considered.

Acting Bug

If you've got the acting bug…get married in a real movie set where real movies are actually made, or a back lot location at Universal Studios. Check www.universalstudios.com or (818) 777-9466 for more details.

The Empire State Building

Tie the knot on top of the once tallest building, the Empire State Building in New York. Stand tall over the big apple.

Beautiful Boat

Say your vows on a beautiful boat with a romantic sunset overlooking the glistening water on the ocean or lake.

Breath of Fresh Air

Take in that fresh mountain air while you say your vows in the wilderness at any number of the beautiful states.

Family Members House

Depending on the size of your guests list, consider marrying in a friend's or family member's house. It could be cost effective and fun.

Visit a National Park

If you enjoy natural beauty, this is the place to say "I do". Yellowstone, Yosemite, Niagara Falls, etc.

Get Married in Your Local Park

Say "I do" in a familiar park, for a magical fairytale setting.

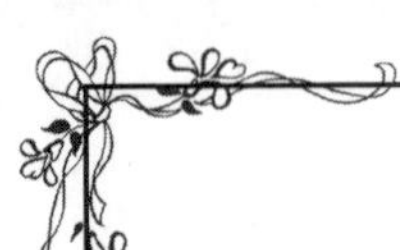

Marry on a Bridge
On your wedding day, have your ceremony on your favorite bridge over the water at sunset.

Picture Perfect Wedding
Be a contemporary bride and groom and marry in your favorite museum. Some museums allow for weddings as well as receptions. Have the wedding invitations reflect the nature of the museum. Such as, if it's an art museum, select a piece from the permanent collection for the outside.

Local Landmark
Look into your favorite landmark or statue to tie the knot.

Reception Hall

Very popular and spacious so let your imagination guide your theme and atmosphere.

Taste of France

If you like French food, try booking a French restaurant for the event.

Take a Wild Ride

Think Knott's Berry Farm. They have a hundred year old chapel, that hosts real ceremonies. You'll have the fun of Knott's to follow and don't forget to bring the kids. Call (714) 220-5074 for more details.

Be a Star

On your wedding day, have your wedding at a location where movies and TV series are filmed. www.amazinglocations.com or call (818) 993-7606 for more details.

Romantic Beach Bluff

Your favorite romantic beach bluff overlooking the ocean or right on the sand. This could range from elegant and romantic to casual and fun.

Crystal Clear Wedding

Get married in the Crystal Cathedral in Garden Grove, CA. (714) 971-4240 for more details.

I'm Going to Disneyland

Have a Fairytale Wedding at the happiest place on earth. Go to their website and they take care of everything.www.disney.com

Ski Chalet

Go to your favorite ski chalet in the winter or summer. A magical experience up in the clouds you'll never forget. This comes complete with a built in honeymoon.

And the Oscar Goes To...the Happy Couple

You are invited to the Academy Awards! Get married in the home of the Academy Awards at the Dorothy Chandler Pavilion in Los Angeles (213) 972-7318. Afterwards, go visit the famous homes of the stars or have dinner at a local restaurant and star search.

Viva Las Vegas Weddings

Go where 120,000 wedding ceremonies are performed each year. Las Vegas weddings are still very popular. They have everything from Elvis weddings, casino weddings, to drive-thru weddings. Join celebrities that have married in Las Vegas from Judy Garland to Elvis Presley, Frank Sinatara, and even Dennis Rodman.

Mall Buff Wedding
How about getting married at the Mall of America's Chapel of Love in Minnesota? Have a wedding and still have time to shop for any last minute items needed from your registry.

Weekend Wedding
Invite guests to stay for the weekend. Include dinners, entertainment with all your guests for a 2-day party until the big day.

Garden-Variety Wedding
Select a venue with a beautiful garden. Have a floral arbor with ivy intertwined. Use as many of the same fragrant flowers to create an unforgettable scent. Decorate the furniture legs with ivy.

Hole in One

Score a hole in one on your favorite golf course, say "I do" and still get in the full 18 holes.

The Love Boat.

Get married on the romantic Love Boat cruise ship and honeymoon at the destination. Ask if the captain will marry you out at sea. Feel like you're king and queen of the world.

On a Rooftop in L.A.

Get married on top of a twelve story building rooftop with a beautiful view of downtown Los Angeles, at The Oviatt Penthouse. www.calendarlive.com/oviatt or (213) 622-6096 for more details. Check locations in other major cities for similar ideas.

Clubhouse Weddings and Receptions

These locations can range from an expensive membership to affordable and fun. They can include golf courses, tennis courts, pools, kitchens and banquet rooms. Or they can be located in your apartment building and available at no cost. It's up to you to turn it into a magical experience.

Princess for a Day
Get married in a castle and feel like a princess for a day. There are many European castles that offer wedding packages and make all the wedding arrangements and even handle all the legal requirements. It's easier than you might think to marry in Europe. There are many books on European weddings.

James Bond 007

Bond enthusiasts can live out their fantasy and tie the knot like her majesty's real British Special Agent. Secretly marry or renew vows at the 007 Bond Street Pub. Bond Gate, Nuneaton, Warwickshire in England Phone: 011 44 1203 347 563. Notify friends and family via a special code announcement. Check marriage license requirements for civil ceremonies in England on the Internet through your consulate. (No legal requirement needed for vow renewals).

Try Your Luck in Atlantic City instead of Las Vegas

Cruise the boardwalk and then say "I Do". See atlanticcity-weddings.com

New York, New York!

Get married at the 94-year-old Plaza Hotel where Catherine Zeta-Jones and Michael Douglas got married. Check for wedding packages and receptions details.

Pier Group Wedding
Marry at the edge of your favorite pier overlooking the glistening water. It comes complete with natural beauty and plenty of onlookers and well wishers.

CLASSIC CARS

Convertible

Double Decker Bus

Rolls Royce

Harley Davidson

MAGICAL Transportation

Make a stylish entrance in a Rolls Royce, or arrive on something less conventional, like a tandem bike. No matter what your budget or your tastes, you'll find something in the following suggestions to elevate your transportation plans from the ordinary to the magical.

Bride and Groom Transportation

Rolls Royce

Exit in high style like the rich and famous.

Limousine

Tinted windows, wedding cake, champagne on ice and a sunroof to give you a grand exit.

Horse and Carriage

This classic touch will be a perfect fairytale addition as you ride off into the sunset together.

Stagecoach

Do as they did a hundred and fifty years ago and depart like you're in the old west.

Hummer

This unusual car has lots of style and can also travel across rugged terrain if need be.

Suburban Limousine

Pack in the wedding party in this new addition to the traditional Lincoln limousine.

Harley Davidson
For those of you who were born to be wild! Your exit on a Harley will be the talk of the town and scandalous. Add a sidecar for more drama.

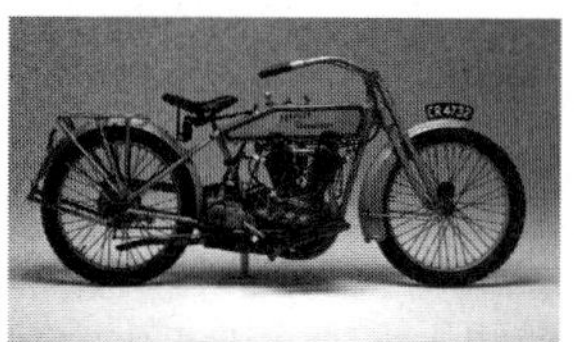

Ferrari or Other High-End Sports Car
Zoom away in a red Ferrari.

Up, Up and Away
Make your exit floating away in a hot air balloon, waving to your guests as you start to go up, up and away.

To Save on Costs
Borrow one of your family or friend's car and ask them to be the driver.

Horse and Wagon
Hop along little doggies as they did many years ago.

Horse and Sleigh
If your wedding is in the winter and you're lucky enough to be in the snow, you have to include a horse and sleigh for the full winter effect.

White Horse
Let the fairytale keep on going, as you leave as the prince and princess on a real white decorated horse.

Tandem Bikes
This is very popular these days. You can depart on a romantic bicycle built for two.

On the Back of a Train
Wave to your respective guests as you leave on a train. Stand at the back and wave good-bye as you begin your new life together.

Trolley or Streetcar Named Desire

If you're tying the knot in an area with streetcars, this is a definite. People will take photos of you and your fifteen minutes of fame will blaze on for a few hours.

Golf Cart

You don't have to be getting married on the golf course to enjoy an exit in a decorated golf cart with cans tied on the rear bumper.

Split a Taxi

For an understated effect to whoosh you off to the airport for your honeymoon, exit in a taxi decorated with "Just Married" sign, flowers, streamers and tin cans.

Transportation for local and out of town guests

Bug a Friend

If you can provide group transportation via buses or mini vans for guests, this would make their day a stress-free, enjoyable event. Ask local guests to assist with the out of town guests for transportation.

Directions

Provide directions and phone numbers for all guests, along with cellular phone numbers, in case anyone gets lost.

Designated Drivers

After the reception, have a group of designated drivers already selected, along with phone numbers of local taxi services.

Sports Car

Let the wind blow in your hair and take life in the fast lane with the top down.

Classic Cars

Jaguar
Mercedes Benz
Model T Ford
Rolls Royce
1957 Chevy

Classic Cars

Looking for some drama? Select a vintage car for some classic style and fun.

Outside At A Vineyard

Scottish Style

Hire a Bagpiper

Prince & Princess For a Day

Ocean Breeze

Theme Weddings

Do you want ocean breezes, a wine tasting event, a fairytale look, or a holiday affair? It's all up to you and your imagination. Why not mix two themes to create a unique and unforgettable memory? Capture it all with a theme wedding and celebrate in your own creative and magical style.

Theme: An Ocean Breeze Beach Wedding

Look and Feel

Cool and casual attire on the beach. Shorts and bare feet are acceptable. Create an arbor made from palm tree fronds. Set surfboards up on the sides. Line the walkway with tikki torches.

Invitations

Create ocean themed invitations including sea life. Fun and casual atmosphere, encouraging a relaxed good time event. Send a shell necklace with your invitations and ask your guest to wear them to the beach wedding.

Locations

Choose your favorite beach bluff overlooking the ocean at sunset to perform the ceremony and have the reception right on the sand.

Colors

Colorful Hawaiian prints

Flowers

Orchids or tropical style flowers

Your Bride and Groom Look

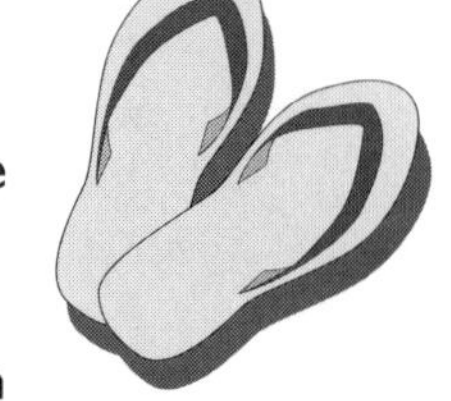

Bride:
Sundress
White pants rolled up with white tank top and veil
Groom:
Khaki shorts or pants, white cotton shirt with tuxedo jacket and tie optional

Bouquet

Simple bouquet of flowing Orchids and tropical flowers.

Ceremony

Write your own vows and have the natural sound of the waves crashing behind you.

Ceremony Music

Bongo drums and guitar

Food

Mexican fiesta, seafood or Hawaiian, coconut shrimp, etc., make it fun.

Cake

White cake with candy sea shells and tropical fresh flowers.

Favors

Plastic sunglasses with wedding couples name and date printed on the frames. Look in your local phone book or check websites for promotional items. Have the photographer get a group shot of everyone with sunglasses at the shoreline.

Theme: Enchanted Evening Wedding

Look and Feel

Mood set with lots of candles, flowers, beautiful music, tulle, and twinkle lights

Invitations

Keep traditional with white paper and black or gold lettering.

Locations

Museum
Clubhouse
Upscale Restaurant
Opera house
Beautiful house

Colors

Black and white

Flowers

Keep it simple, but elegant
Casablanca Lilies
Red velvet roses
Lily of the Valley

Your Bride and Groom Look

Classic and traditional.

Bouquet

Snow white roses with lily of the valley, tied with a white satin ribbon.

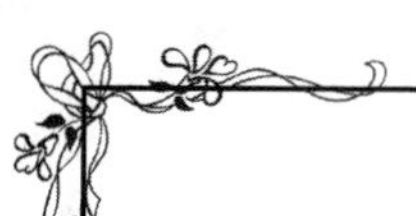

Ceremony

"Heavenly White". A truly romantic touch is to have white branches with white twinkle lights and tulle to create an arbor where you'll be doing your vows. Use up-lights to heighten the room and set the mood. Include twinkle lights in potted shrubs with rose petals scattered down the isle. Instead of bouquets, have your wedding party carry candles. A magical effect coming down the aisle.

Ceremony Music

Three string quartet

Reception

Large crystal bowls overflowing with fresh strawberries. Place a small bowl of white and dark chocolate for dipping. Keep chocolate warm with small tea candle in glass candleholders as warmers. *Be careful with the candles.* Keep everything white. Use white table linens, white dishes, and for the napkins, roll up and tie with white satin ribbon and include a sprig of rosemary. The color will come from the centerpiece crystal bowl of strawberries. Ice sculptures would certainly add a beautiful touch to an evening wedding.

Food

Passed hors d' oeuvres.

Cake

White cake with simple white shaved chocolate and fresh flowers. Keep it simple and elegant.

Theme: Prince and Princess for a day "Fairytale Wedding"

Look and Feel

Whimsical and magical, everything and your fairy godmother.

Invitations

Engraved on pure white or ivory paper, printed in script.

Locations

Large ballroom to accommodate a waltz style dance floor.

Colors

White, Light Blue, Pale Pink, Gold

Your Bride and Groom Look

A fairytale princess big full skirt, white of course, with a tiara. Include a pair of "Glass" slippers - don't worry they're not glass (found in most bridal stores). Groom to wear a tux with tails, a top hat and gloves.

Bouquet

Choose a large spring bouquet with baby's breath and flowing ivy to complete the look.

Ceremony

Select a horse drawn carriage with white horse to take you from the ceremony to the reception. Have your young ring bearer carry a real crystal glass slipper on top of a purple velvet pillow with wedding rings inside.

Ceremony Music

Classical music, four piece quartet or classical guitarist and violin.

Cake

At the cake table, include silver glitter on the white linens to set the magical mood. Include a castle figurine or glass carriage for a topper on the cake.

Favors

Miniature glass slippers filled with candies.

Reception

Include white tulle sprinkled with glitter and white candles in hurricane lamps, and with small pumpkins throughout for the real fairytale effect.
When leaving the church, drift away into the sunset in a hot air balloon.
For a finishing touch to this magical day, have an ice sculpture made of a glass slipper.

Theme: Spring is in the Air "French Country"

Look and Feel

This fun, romantic theme is perfect for a springtime wedding. Create a fresh, festive floral ambience accompanied with white benches and white tables topped with brightly colored French motif patterns. Elegant in style, yet relaxed country comfort.

Invitations

Spray a floral scented perfume onto the invitations. Use a script or curly typestyle. Make your own invitations and glue a flat dried flower at the top or bottom. Include a famous French wedding phrase at the top or bottom (check internet for verbage).

Locations

Try to select a venue with a garden. Have a floral arbor with ivy intertwined. Use as many of the same fragrant flowers to create an unforgettable scent. Decorate the furniture legs with ivy. Sprinkle small flowers down the aisle. The tables should have fresh flowers as a centerpiece.

Colors

Mix patterns, such as floral with stripes.
Pink, White, Blue, Periwinkle, Yellow

Flowers

Arrange your fresh cutting flowers to include large Sunflowers, Daisies, Babies Breath, Casablanca Lilies, Roses, Stargazers, and Gardenias.

Your Bride and Groom Look

Brides wear flowers in your hair. Perhaps the flowers could be a crown or woven at the top. If hats

are your style, wear some fresh flowers on the brim or side of the hat. For the groom, wear a black and gray vest with pin stripes or wear a floral vest or cummerbund with a fresh baby rose as boutonnière.

Bouquet
Loose bouquet with various flowers tied with a simple but elegant satin ribbon

Ceremony
Release butterflies at the end of the ceremony.

Ceremony Music
Classical with violins and cellos

Food
Include various French cheeses such as Munster and Camembert with French wine and champagne. Also have fresh baguettes at each table in a basket with butter. Provance style foods from the south of France with beef or fish, spring vegetables, etc. Check the Internet for menus.

Cake
White shaved chocolate frosting on cake to include different flavors on each tier. Decorate the outside with fresh spring flowers.

Favors
Miniature baskets with a selection of potpourri sachets in lace, French chocolates, miniature bottle of wine, cheese and crackers, tea, chocolate, French coffee cordials, flower seed packets symbolizing growth and future with the wedding date and couples name, mints, etc.

Theme: Happy New Year Wedding

Look and Feel

Here's a way to have all your friends already dressed up and ready to party. The champagne is already flowing at this celebration.

Invitations

Be different and have a martini-shaped invitation.

Locations

Select the grand ballroom of a local hotel.

Colors

Silver, Black

Your Bride and Groom Look

Cocktail party formal

Bouquet

White roses tied with a silver ribbon.

Ceremony

How about a surprise wedding at midnight? Let everyone think they are just going to another New Year's Eve party. You know everyone is staying until midnight. Don't tell anyone you'll be tying the knot and at midnight let the wedding ceremony begin. This is great for second marriages.

Ceremony Music

Bring a CD of one of your favorite groups or singer. Simple popular songs played in the background.

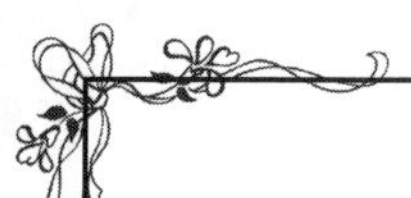

Food
New Year's Eve party food.

Cake
Use sparklers on top of the cake.

Favors
Sound makers with bride and groom's name imprinted, along with wedding date.

Reception
Confetti, sound makers, balloons and party hats. Have all the necessities at each table. Your tables will be ready- decorated with the theme.

Theme: It's in the Air - Christmas!

Look and Feel

Staying warm for winter and snuggling up. Everything will be beautifully lit for the holidays and this gives you one less thing to think about. The setting is complete.

Invitations

White with embossed lettering.

Locations

Go to your favorite ski chalet, beautiful mansion, or estate that is decorated for the holidays.

Colors

Burgundy, Hunter Green
White and gold

Flowers

An ideal choice is Poinsettias. White, pink or red.

Your Bride and Groom Look

Play up the holidays and have a white velvet dress and cape.
For your groom, keep him simply done up in a traditional black tuxedo with a mistletoe boutonnière. If you want to go more with a casual winter holiday wedding, the men can wear nice wool sweates,, and slacks. Brides, you can tone down your look by wearing white cashmere, dressed up with pearls.

Bouquet

Any white flowers with ivy flowing.

Ceremony

Have Christmas music playing softly in the background as guests are being seated. Be sure to include a beautifully lit Christmas tree. If there are no gifts under the tree, add some wrapped boxes. Create a real winter wonderland; if you're in the snow leave the ceremony in a white horse-drawn sleigh.

Ceremony Music

Christmas music is a must
Strolling carolers
Local choir

Food

Christmas feast. Turkey with stuffing and all the trimmings.
Hot apple cider
Hot chocolate

Cake

White cake on a table dressed up with white batting or large sheets of fluffy cotton, scattered fresh Christmas tree trimmings and white twinkle lights. Include cute little village houses lit from inside to really create the mood.

Favors

Buy some beautiful ornaments and write your names and wedding date for everyone to take, or Christmas snow globes.

Theme: Theme "J' adore Paris"

Look and Feel

European, cosmopolitan, elegant yet simple.

Invitations

Dark blue, black and gold colors. Perhaps engrave a silver or gold foil stamp of the new last name initial in a reversed-out circle at the top of the invitation. Use a French script typestyle and select French phrases that would be appropriate. "Joyeux de Vivre" - joy of life "Vivre la (couples name)" - long live (couples name)

Locations

If you are near a local winery, set up a wine tasting event at the reception. Weather permitting, tie the knot outside near the vineyard itself. Scout a gothic style church for the wedding and have a little renaissance imagery added at the reception. Imagery ideas such as; urns with moss, a parchment scrolled guest book with crow quill pen and ink, a charcoal portrait of the couple in a gold frame at the entrance, a violinist or classical guitarist at entrance as well.

Reception

Depending on the size, a house, reception hall or perhaps a French restaurant with catering capabilities. Play background French folk music while the guests are dinning.

Colors
Blue,White, Red ,Gold, Black, Silver

Flowers
Giant Sunflowers or fragrant selection including, Lily of the Valley, Gardenias and Casablanca Lilies.

Your Bride and Groom Look
Groom to wear simple tuxedo with tails with the bride wearing a simple white dress, long or short.

Bouquet
Simple bouquet of a bunch of Lily of the Valley tied at the bottom with a dark green satin ribbon.

Ceremony
Classic and elegant.

Ceremony Music
Four piece quartet.

Reception
Have several different varieties of French wines. Hire a wine enthusiast to pour and give a little bit of their knowledge of these wines from the beautiful French wine country.

Hors d'oeuvres should include, miniature croissants and quiches, escargot, Brie and various spreads and baguettes.

On the tables have selections of Pate-Brie and baskets of baguettes

For dessert have selections of Crème Brule, French Petifours, Grand Marnier Crepe Bar, traditional Apple flavored Ice Cream, and of course, Café au lait and Cappuccino.

Hire a couple of artists to set up easels and do quick watercolors of your guests.

Have a strolling violinist or an accordionist to play classic French songs.

Hire a professional actor to play the maitre 'd and entertain guests as they enter.

Favors
Give your guests a small bottle of French wine with your own custom designed label from wine.com.

Food
Serve the meal in a style that reflects great cuisine with great presentation. You could have it catered by a local French restaurant. Many times there are actual French countrymen working there who will contribute to the ambience.

Theme: "Be My Valentine" Valentines Day

Look and Feel

Hearts and love are in the air. Cupid and arrows, pink and red with candy hearts.

Invitations

Any type invitations that include a heart, Cherubs, and Angels also give the feel. Handmade papers with pressed flowers. Sprinkle a little red heart confetti or some potpourri inside each invitation (not too much though).

Locations

Favorite Italian restaurant
A wine vineyard
Cute bed and breakfast

Colors

Pink or Red
White

Flowers

Red and white roses

Your Bride and Groom Look

Wear tiny pink roses in your hair
Traditional white wedding dress with ruby red earrings or necklace

Bouquet
Red, white and pink roses with a satin, deep red ribbon, tied with long tails.

Ceremony
Garden arbor with lots of flowers, and guests to sit in white chairs that are decorated with fresh nosegays tied to the top. Have the flower girl dressed like a fairy sprinkling fresh flowers down the aisle.

Ceremony Music
String quartet

Reception
Include bowls of chocolates or tiny heart-shaped candies.

Food
Champagne with strawberries submerged into the glass
Pink champagne with colored sugar around the rim
Non-alcoholic Shirley Temples, be sure to include the cherries
Pink lemonade

Cake
Sprinkle the cake table with tiny heart-shaped candies

Favors
Hershey kisses wrapped in a tulle bag and tied with a red satin ribbon
Gourmet chocolates
Heart box filled with candies

Theme: Vineyard Wedding

Look and Feel

Romantic setting in a country vineyard-- great wine included.

Invitations

Hear it through the grapevine. Parchment paper with grapevines and calligraphy writing

Locations

Next to the vineyard on a beautiful hillside

Colors

Purple and gold

Flowers

Include grape leaves in the flowers you select

Your Bride and Groom Look

Off-white simple wedding dress and the groom to wear a black fitted suit with simple tie.

Bouquet

White roses and grapevine twined through

Ceremony

Late afternoon, and outdoors

Music

4 piece band

Food
Wine tasting with assorted cheeses, fresh fruit and crackers
Gourmet pizza and pasta bar

Cake
Decorate with grape leaves and grapes
Favors:
Bottle of wine with your own personalized label

Ring Bearer Carries Glass Slipper

ELECTRIC GUITAR SOLO

Sunrise Wedding

Surprise Ceremony

Fireworks

MAGICAL

Ceremony Ideas

Picture yourself a radiant bride walking down the aisle. The music swells to greet you. Your fiancé, and friends and family are holding their breaths in excitement. Does just thinking about it give you goose bumps? Or do you have something completely different in mind? Well, let the performance begin! But first, ask yourself a few questions. What mood do you want to convey? What time of year will the ceremony take place, and will it be indoors or out? Will the ceremony be religious? How many people will attend? What kind of music will you play? As the conductor of your wedding, you get to decide every detail. To help you focus your ideas, here's a list of suggestions - ranging from the general to the specific. Use them to design the day you have always dreamed of, and make your magical performance one to remember.

Photograph Moment

Ask the photographer to have the groom wait for the bride. Simply have the groom turned around when the bride comes out for the photo. Coordinate with the photographer to photograph the first impression of the groom when he sees his bride for the first time…a magical moment!

Rose Petal Walkway

Line the walkway with fresh Rose petals for a sophisticated and romantic setting.

Be a Star for a Day

Feel like a celebrity as you enter the church or place of worship. Place a red carpet on the walkway.

Star Attraction

Rent a large flood light and place near the reception for a night time special event look. Feel like a Hollywood celebrity.

Horse Dawn Carriage

Have a horse drawn carriage take you from the ceremony to the reception (use white horses for a fairytale effect)

Magical Aroma

To spruce up a floral bouquet and decorations, add rosemary, cut lemons, and a romantic grapevine to the arrangements for a magical aroma.

Holiday Decorations

If you have a winter wedding, the place of worship may already be decorated for the holidays, giving you a head start.

Autumn Wedding

For an autumn wedding, decorate with white roses and autumn leaves for a truly magical effect.

Upbeat Pop Song

Add some fun and a special touch into a long and mellow ceremony by inserting an upbeat pop song in the middle to enliven your guests.

Mix it Up

For a whimsical effect to your motif, mix patterns, such as florals with stripes.

Horse Drawn Sleigh

Create a real winter wonderland and depart the ceremony with a white horse drawn sleigh.

Calligraphy Marriage License

Instead of the basic marriage license, have a calligrapher reproduce the wording using beautiful lettering on handmade paper. This will be what you and your new husband sign along with the officiate. Your marriage license is now beautiful enough to frame and hang.

A Surprise Wedding at Midnight

Let everyone think they are just going to another New Year's Eve party. You know everyone is staying until midnight. Don't tell anyone you'll be tying the knot at midnight, then let the wedding ceremony begin.

New Twist to "Here Comes the Bride"

Instead of the traditional *HERE COMES THE BRIDE*, walk down the isle to an upbeat popular song of a selected era, or simply your favorite song.

Let the Guitar Strum

Consider a live electric guitar solo of *HERE COMES THE BRIDE* as you glide down the aisle in contemporary fashion. Or hire a violinist and a classical guitar accompanyment to set a classical mood.

Have Balloons Released

After the ceremony, include the colors of your theme and the bride and groom's name imprinted on the balloons, and let them fly.

White Branches and Twinkle Lights

A truly romantic touch is to have white branches with white twinkle lights and tulle to create an arbor where you'll be exchanging your vows.

Set the Mood

Use up-lights to heighten the drama and set the mood for an evening wedding.

Potted Shrubs Lit Up

Have twinkle lights in potted shrubs lining the walkway.

Evening Wedding

Your wedding party carries candles instead of traditional flowers, as well as, line the aisle with small candles. This effect would be very magical and dramatic.

Smile!

After your minister pronounces you husband and wife, have a small camera handy and turn around and tell your guests to "smile" as you want to have a picture of all of them from the alter. - Great wedding photo idea!

Sunrise Wedding

Why not. Have a morning ceremony and buffet brunch. This would be magical, especially atop a volcano in Hawaii as the sun peaks over the ocean. Then take a helicopter ride around the island while drinking champagne. Then relax the rest of the day by the pool or on the beach.

Winter Wedding

Include artificial snow and glitter sprinkled down the walkway.

A Bit of History

In your wedding program under each attendant's name, include how long he or she has known the bride and groom. Perhaps a photo as children together and a fun story about their friendship.

Ceremony Butterflies, Literally

Have monarch butterflies released after the ceremony when you are leaving the church to signify good luck. Floridamonarch.com

Let the White Doves Fly

Have white birds released after the ceremony.

Face your Guests

When the bride and groom arrive at the alter, position them facing the guests instead of facing the minister. This way the guests can see the bride and groom during the ceremony.

Famous Writers Hang Out
One couple interviewed said they got married at the AlGonquin Round Table Restaurant in New York since the bride was a writer. This is where famous writers were known to visit in the 20's; Dorothy Park, and Robert Benchley were part of the round table. Select from any of your favorite restaurants and be married while having breakfast, lunch or dinner by a judge. They did it, and said this was very inexpensive and fun. They wouldn't have done anything different.

Ceremony Surprise
In your program, don't give all the details about the wedding, everyone will be following along. This way everyone will relax and watch the ceremony, not knowing what to expect next.

Wedding Acknowledgements
Include wedding acknowledgements in your wedding program and a "thank you" to the parents.

Ask your Mother or Grandmother
Ask either your mother or grandmother to be in your Wedding Party. Start a tradition for your children or grandchildren.

Here Comes the Judge
For an inexpensive creative ceremony, arrange for a Judge to meet you at your favorite venue. Choose from a famous bridge, park, pier or beach, etc. You choose the magic for this location.

Fireworks Show
If possible in your area, see if you can arrange a spectacular fireworks display after the ceremony in the evening.

Glass Slipper or a Crown
Have your young ring bearer carry a real crystal glass slipper or a crown on top of a purple velvet pillow including the rings.

Fairytale Flower Girl

Dress your flower girl up as a cute fairy to complete the look. A balerina outfit will do in a pinch.

Greet the Guests

After the ceremony, the bride and groom greets each row of the guests on their way out of the chapel.

Scottish Theme

Ask the groom to get married in a kilt and hire bagpipers to play. See if the entire wedding party will be willing to wear kilts. Hire a Scottish minister.

Throw Some Lavender

Encourage guests to throw fresh lavender in prepackaged sachets.

Include a Harpist

Include a harpist to play during your ceremony for a heavenly effect.

Bring your Favorite Flower

In your wedding invitations, ask guests to bring a single stem of their favorite flower. Once they arrive for the ceremony, instruct the guests to place their flower in the arbor as a blessing for the bride and groom.

Moonlight Wedding

In the warm summer months, check your calendar for the full moons. Have your wedding on the night of a full moon, and let the moon be your romantic lighting for the evening.

Autumn Wedding Leaves

Sprinkle leaves, that have turned the beautiful autumn colors, down the walkway.

Maid of Honor Reads Vows

Romantic Poetry

Hire a Copywriter

Sing Your Vows

Write a Song

Vows

The exchange of vows can be one of the most romantic moments in the wedding ceremony. It can also be one of the most traumatic moments for those of us with a fear of public speaking. Don't worry. Even if you're not a wordsmith, you will sound like a romantic, seventeenth century, French poet by simply speaking words that come from the heart. Well before the ceremony, sit down and write out the vows you'd express to your loved one if he or she were sitting right next to you. Perhaps you could begin by thanking his or her parents for raising such a wonderful son or daughter and making this moment possible. Perhaps you'd like your vows to reflect your religious beliefs, or have a cute and playful theme. Still not sure what to say? As you read through the following suggestions, look for ideas that speak to you and then add, mix, match, and modify them, until they are uniquely yours.

Write a romantic poem to each other.

Poems
Have the officiant read a selected poem to the both of you.

Romantic Poetry
Stroll through the library and browse the section of romantic poetry. If you don't have a favorite poet, open up any poetry book, at any chapter and verse and see if that author has the style you are seeking.

Popular Poets
To reference; Pablo Neruda, William Shakespeare, Robert Browning, Rod McKuen, E.E. Cummings, John Keats.

Search the Web
If you have access to the Internet, it's a great resource for romantic words and phrases.

Include Your Own Words in the Ceremony
Give the officiant your scripted vows to review a few weeks before the wedding day (if possible). Ask if your scripted vows could be tailored to the overall marriage ceremony. Why not choose three words to be the overall theme such as love, understanding and communication. Have the officiant work in your vows for a blended union that's relative to each of you.

Be Prepared

Keep a handkerchief in the groom's jacket pocket just in case your beautiful wedding vows overwhelm you.

Simple Phrases

Remember a few words or a simple phrase from your wedding vows, so in the coming years, you can easily add them on cards or messages to your mate and to conjure up the romance of the good times remembered.

Focus on Your Partner

When exchanging vows, remember to focus on your partner, because you are the only two people in the world right then and there.

Bridal and Groomsmen Readings

If you just can't bring yourself to say the vows yourself, have your best man, maid of honor or even the one giving the ceremony say them for you. It could be very emotional to have another person read something so personal while you are looking into your partner's eyes. It is similar to hearing your inner thoughts or a voiceover in a movie.

Practice Makes Perfect
Practice saying your vows to yourself, friends and family, and your delivery will be more natural.

Print Your Vows
If you have a simple program for the event, print your vows so others can hear and read the exchange.

Sing a Song
Sing your favorite song to each other from a famous musical or play.

Write a Song to your Mate
Have the song played by a professional musician at the appropriate time.

Framed for Future Memories
Have your romantic vows written down in script or calligraphy and framed for a personal reminder of the feelings that originally brought you two together.

Hire a Copywriter
If all else fails and you still want those special vows, hire a copywriter to write what you feel. It probably will be inexpensive and certainly less time consuming. Look in the phonebook, or on the internet for a list of copywriters in your area.

How you Knew This Was It

For your wedding vows, describe in brief detail the time you knew that this was that special person and someday you would marry.

Celebrate Your Heritage

Translate your vow or a popular phrase from that country as part of your vows.

Thank the Parents

Thank the parents for having, and allowing you the opportunity to marry, their son or daughter.

Relate a Humorous Anecdote

Tell a little humorous story about the first time you met, emphasizing the importance of laughter in the life of your marriage. Light laughter will put everyone at ease and minimize any faux pas.

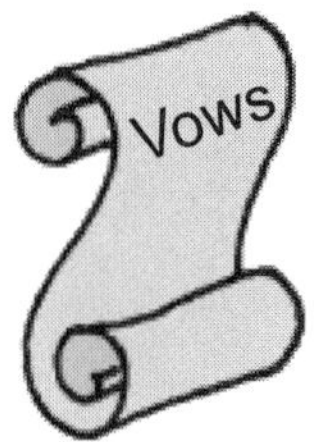

POEMS

Let me not to the marriage of true minds
Admit impediments. Love is not love
Which alters when it alteration finds
Or bends with the remover to remove.
O, no, it is an ever fixed mark
That looks on tempests and is never shaken,
It is the star to every wandering bark,
Whose worth's unknown, although his height be taken.
Love's not time's fool, though rosy lips and cheeks
Within his bending sickle's compass come,
Love alters not with his brief hours and weeks,
But bears it out even to the edge of doom
If this be error, and upon me proved,
I never writ, nor no man ever loved.

From "Sonnet 116," in Love Poems and Sonnets of William Shakespeare:

Come live with me and be my love,
And we will all the pleasures prove
That valleys, groves, hills and fields,
Woods, or steepy mountain yields.
And we will sit upon the rocks,
Seeing the shepherds feed their flocks,
By shallow rivers to whose falls
Melodious birds sing madrigals.

And I will make thee beds of roses
And a thousand fragrant posies,
A cap of flowers, and a kirtle
Embroidered all with leaves of myrtle;

A gown made of the finest wool
Which from our pretty lambs we pull;
Fair lined slippers for the cold,
With buckles of the purest gold;

A belt of straw and ivy buds,
With coral clasps and amber studs:
And if these pleasures may thee move,
Come live with me, and be my love.

The shepherds' swains shall dance and sing
For thy delight each May morning;
If these delights thy mind may move,
Then live with me and be my love.
-- Christopher Marlowe

Include some of the following in your vows as options.

I commit to loving you, protect and encourage you, be your honest best friend, and remain with you no matter what the circumstance, as long as we both shall live.

I hereby promise in front of these witnesses here today to declare my love and faithfulness from now until eternity.

I hereby declare my love and respect to you, and look forward to sharing my emotions and interests through life's experiences, including joyous times along with a commitment always and forever.

I will always be your loyal and ardent confidante, to share dreams, secrets and hopes for the future.

From "How Do I Love Thee?", by Elizabeth Barrett Browning in One Hundred and One Classic Love Poems:

How do I love thee? Let me count the ways
I love thee to the depth and breadth and height
My soul can reach

you are my best friend and the one I want to share my life with.
I will love you forever, and under all circumstances.
I will stand by you always.
I will have faith in you and encourage you in everything you do.
I will be here to listen to you, to laugh with you, and to hold you.
I will work with you as we build a life together,
And I will support you as you live your own independent life.
I will strive every day to make our relationship stronger.
I will be your friend, your love, and your partner for all the days of our lives.

Sample Vows

Here are some romantic vows to use or to jump-start your own creativity:

"There is no other person that could have captured my heart the way you have. You simply take my breath away and I look forward to sharing our wonderful future together."

"Since we met, my life has been an abundance of romance and happiness up to this special moment. And hereafter, when we write life's chapters, I promise to be your loving _____, trusted partner and loyal friend, forever and always."

"Words cannot express the way I feel about you on this special day, so I only wish to convey that I will honor, cherish and be your loving and life partner always."

On this special day, I unite my life to yours.
From this special day forward, I vow to be your partner
and loyal best friend.
I cherish the joy we discover in each other's successes,
as well as the ones we share together,
and shield you from any obstacles you may encounter,
I will always be there for you, whether good or bad.
Your happiness is my happiness
as we grow together because we deserve the best from each other.
I promise to listen and support you when you are in doubt,
comfort and protect you in bad times,
and be your pillar of strength in uncertain times.
I will be loyal and honest always,
and adore you forever.
This is my vow to you.

I, (Bride's Name), take (you), (Groom's Name),
to be my husband,
secure in the knowledge that you will be
my eternal best friend,
my faithful and loving partner,
and my one true love always.
On our special wedding day today,
I give to you in the presence of God and these witnesses
my sacred commitment to stay beside you as your faithful wife and friend in sickness and in health, in happier times as well as the bad.
I promise to love you completely, protect you in times of trouble,
support you with your goals, laugh, cry and grow with you,
and will always cherish our relationship forever.

Mistletoe Boutonnière

BUTTERFLIES IN YOUR HAIR

Glass Slippers

Barefoot on the Beach

MAGICAL

Bride & Groom Attire

You are what you wear. Brides, choose clothing that expresses your own personal style whether it's a fairytale ball gown or a sleek, sophisticated, white dress. Grooms, nowadays anything is acceptable, from a traditional black tuxedo, to a wool sweater and slacks, to full period clothing. Choose your attire to complement your wedding's theme or style and let the magic begin.

Brides

Dazzling Hat

Hats are wonderful for dressing up your style. For a summer wedding, feel like royalty and wear a dazzling hat. You're sure to be the princess of the ball.

Fairytale Glass Slippers

To get the real "fairytale" effect you can now buy shoes at most bridal stores that look like glass slippers. (don't worry, they're really not glass)

Check e-bay

For wedding dresses, go to the internet on www.e-bay.com to check for great pricing. You will be amazed.

Memories of Your Grandmother

Wear a magical memento, from a grandmother or great grandmothers, like a pin or pendant.

Tiny Butterflies in Your Hair

Tiaras are in, along with faux gems that look like tiny butterflies and flowers, to light up your hair.

Fairytale Princess Big Full Skirt

Complete the fairytale look, by wearing a magical dress with a full skirt.

Play up the Holidays

If you're planning a holiday theme, wear a white velvet dress and cape.

Stay Warm

Wear a pashmina cashmere shawl, the colors are beautiful and will be a nice addition to your winter wedding.

Keep it Cool
Sundresses are a perfect look for a summer or beach wedding.

Somewhere in Time Look
Capture the look of the Victorian era with romantic hat, gloves and strolling parasol.

Beach Bride
White pants rolled up with white tank top and veil.

Extra Tulle on Your Veil
Include a long trail of tulle to your veil.

Break in Your Wedding Shoes
Wear your wedding day shoes to break them in before the big day.

Brides Wear Fresh Flowers in Your Hair
Perhaps the flowers could be a crown or woven at the top. If hats are your style, wear fresh or dried flowers somewhere on the brim or side of the hat.

New Colors
Select a different color instead of traditional white for your bridal gown.

Reception Comfort

Have a pair of white tennis shoes for the reception. Switch out of those uncomfortable great looking heels, so you'll be comfortable for all your dancing and socializing.

Groom

White Tuxedo Jacket

If it's a summer wedding, the groom could wear a white tuxedo jacket with black pants.

A Tux With Tails

Capture the old fashioned glamour with a tux and tails.

Beach Groom

Khaki shorts or pants, white cotton shirt with tuxedo jacket and tie optional.

Casual Winter Wedding

If you want to go for the casual winter holiday feel, guys can wear nice wool sweaters and slacks.

Victorian Groom

Black and gray vest with pin stripes or wear a floral vest or cummerbund and a dried baby rose as boutonniere.

Tailored, Fitted Suit
Instead of the traditional tux, buy a new tailored, fitted suit.

Hip Look
Include a monochromatic shirt and tie scheme with your tuxedo instead of black and white.

Tie One On
Wear a tie with a pattern instead of a bow tie and include cuff links for regal effect.

Picture Perfect to the Bride
Have boutonnieres made for the groom using the same flowers that are in the brides bouquet. If your wedding is during the summer, have two made in case one of them starts to wilt.

Mistletoe Boutonnière

If you're planning a winter wedding, have the groom wear a mistletoe boutonnière.

Wear a Tiara

To every little girl in each of us, a glittering tiara on the bride, says "princess".

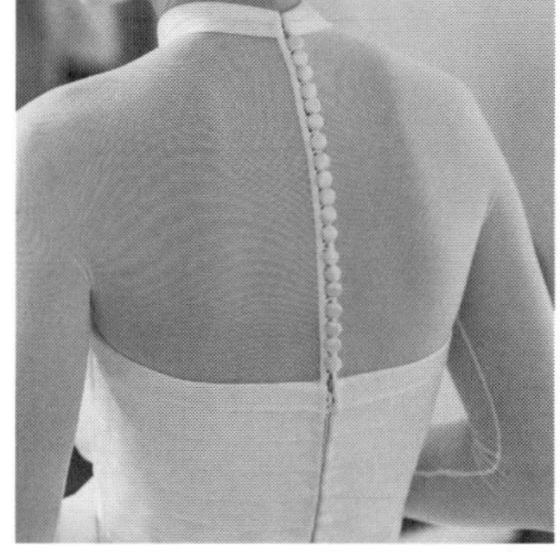

A tiara is a wonderful idea to enhance the sophistication and magical effect of your dress.

Flower Girls

Renaissance Look

Turn your cute little flower girls into fair maidens for the day and dress them as part of a Renaissance theme.

Keep Your Flower Girl in Style with the Wedding

Dress your flower girls to compliment the style of the wedding. Include beautiful fabrics with pretty ribbons, covered buttons and flowers in their hair.

Flower girls will be the magical special addition everyone will appreciate.

Children's Menus

French Crepe Bar

SUSHI BAR

Giant Salad Bar

Paella & Sangria

Catering Ideas

What's for dinner, lunch, or brunch? Depending on your budget, you can serve a five-course dinner feast, or a simple evening meal with hors d'oeuvres and champagne. Hoping to get away from serving traditional chicken of fish dishes? Looking for foods that interest children? As you browse throug the following list of suggestions, you'll find an elaborate selection of culinary styles to chose from to create your magical meal.

Spanish Style

Paella and sangria with tapas appetizers including chicken croquettes, empanadas, Spanish tortillas, garlic shrimp, olives and montego cheese.

New Orleans Style Cajun

Jambalaya, cajun popcorn, dirty rice, fried catfish and cornbread.

Carving Station

Carved tenderloin, roast beef or turkey with butter rolls, fresh cranberry sauce. Ham with buttermilk biscuits and butter.

French Pate'

Assortment of pate' including champagne, vegetable and fish. Include select cheeses such as brie and Gruyere served with assorted mustards, cornichons and crusty French baguettes. Assorted vegetables. Fresh assortment of seasonal vegetables with various dips.

French Crepes

Crepes filled with ham, seafood, and vegetables and for dessert include fruit and liqueur (Grand Marinier).

Chinese Dishes

Hot and sour soup or egg drop. Kung pao chicken, or beef with assorted fried rice dishes.

World Curry

Beef, chicken, lamb or vegetable curry with rice and shredded coconut.

Hawaiian Style

Roasted pig served with pineapple mango sauce and coconut rice and Maui onion rings. Served with rice and mango sauce topped with a fresh orchid.

Mexican Style

Grilled chicken and beef Fajitas served on flour or corn tortillas with guacamole, onions, tomato, three Mexican cheeses and salsa.

Greek Selections

Baba ghanoush, stuffed grape leaves, humus and falafel. Served with pita bread.

Moroccan Delight
Beef, lamb or chicken, and olives. Served with pita bread.

New York, New York Style Deli
Pastrami, Corn Beef, and Turkey with rye and pumpernickel breads with dill pickles and cole slaw.

Lotsa Pasta Bar
Pasta bar staffed with a chef preparing fresh pasta with various sauces including, fresh tomato basil, Alfredo and pesto. Served with Italian garlic bread sticks.

Giant Salad Bar
European greens, edible flowers served with an olive oil/balsamic vinegar dressing. Toppings of cherry tomatoes, hot house cucumbers, parmesan cheese, artichoke hearts, bacon bits, avocado and red green, orange and yellow peppers.

Seafood Fest
Large shrimp and Alaskan king crab legs with hot, drawn garlic butter and/or cocktail sauce. Include oyster shooters and oysters on the half shell.

Southern Comfort Food
Catfish fish fry and real Southern fried chicken, Jack Daniels barbecued ribs, biscuits and gravy, hush puppies and okra salad.

Sushi Bar

Include a Japanese sushi chef preparing Sushi and Sashimi to order. Include some of the basics such as Miso soup, California rolls, crunchy rolls, hand rolls, spicy rolls and teriyaki chicken with white rice and vegetables.

Coffee Station

At the end of the evening, before their long drive home, offer a coffee station with flavored coffees, decaf, an assortment of fine teas, an espresso bar and assorted cookies for your guests.

Children's Menu

Pizzas
Hot Dogs
Hamburgers and French fries
Spaghetti
Grilled cheese sandwiches
Chicken fingers

Children's Desserts

Ice Cream Cones
Fun Shape Cookies
Cup Cakes
Caramel Apples
Assorted Candies
Vanilla & Chocolate Pudding
Pink Lemonade & Kool-Aid

Caramel Apples

Pizza

Cookies

CHICKEN FINGERS

Dancing On A Cloud

Sugared Champagne Glasses

SKYWRITING

Hire An Actor

Monte Carlo Casino

Reception Ideas

PARTY! The mood is set, you've just given the performance of a lifetime, and all that's left to do is bask in the spotlight and celebrate. The wedding reception is where you can most express your personality. Throw the bash of the century for hundreds of people, or throw aside convention and create a celebration for two by sharing a romantic evening alone in an Italian castle, or relaxing together on the beach. What appeals to you? Your choices are endless, which is why the process of deciding is so much fun, but can seem overwhelming at the same time. The following ideas are designed to help you explore some of the creative options available to you, and to stimulate your own ideas. Remember, it's your party. Do what pleases you most and have the magical event of the millennium.

Guest Registry

Place a large scroll of paper at the entrance with colored pencils or fountain pen for guests to sign as they enter.

Sign on Matt of Photo

Place an enlarged engagement photo, with wide matting and pen, for everyone to sign.

English Theme

Place tall topiary centerpieces on each table.

Chocolate or Strawberry Initials or Hearts

On the dessert plates, ask your caterer to squirt your names, initials or a heart in either chocolate, white chocolate or strawberry preserves to be served with each guest's slice of wedding cake.

Cut the Cake

When it's time to cut the cake at the reception, have a different flavored cake at each guest's table with a cutting knife. Once the cutting of the main cake is complete, guests will already have their cake at the table and, they can cut their own piece. The cake also serves as a centerpiece.

Picture History

Have a large format picture printed of a collage of pictures of the bride. Include baby pictures, childhood, dating to pre-wedding. It will be fun for everyone to see before they enter the reception.

Folk Music
Play background cultural folk music while the guests dine to accompany the theme and food.

Hire a Wine Connoisseur
Have several different varieties of wines. Hire a wine connoisseur to pour and share a little bit of their knowledge on these wines from the wine country.

Picnic
On each guest's table, have a bottle of wine and selections of pate', brie and baskets of baguettes atop a checkered table cloth to give the feel of a French country picnic.

Candlesticks
To enhance the romance of candlesticks, place fresh flowers at the base of them.

Sugared Champagne Glasses
Wet the top of the champagne glasses and dip them into colored sugars for a magical colored effect.

Hire an Actor
Contact Premiere Speakers at 800-296-2336 to arrange a famous actor to make a special appearance on your special day.

Delay Cutting the Cake

If you want your guests to stay a little longer, delay the cake cutting until you're ready for the reception to wind down.

Stroling Violinist

Hire a stroling violinist or an accordionist to play music for your theme wedding.

Hire an Actor

Hire a professional actor to play a French Maitre d and entertain guests as they enter.

Artistic Guests

At the reception, have a large canvas with paintbrushes and water base paint. Ask your guests to paint something. After the wedding you'll have an original piece of artwork that will remind you of your big day.

Candles

Include lots of candles and French urns for a truly romantic feel.

Light My Fire
Tiki Torches are popular with beach weddings... you can dress them with bows and starfish.

Beautiful Reception Chairs
Drape bridal tulling around a basic chair and tie at the center with a big satin ribbon. Insert fresh cut flowers through the bow in the back for that magic touch.

Menu Cards
Place a beautifully done menu card at each table, announcing appetizers, main course and dessert. This way your guests will know exactly what they can expect.

Hot Pretzels and Popcorn
As your guests are leaving the reception, have a hot pretzel and popcorn station with cold sodas for their drive home.

Sealing Wax Place Cards
To create a European feel on your place cards, next to the guest's name put sealing wax and the first initial of your last name.

Bowl of Strawberries

Place large crystal bowls overflowing with fresh strawberries. Place small bowls of white and dark chocolate for dipping. Keep chocolate warm with a small tea candle in glass candleholders as warmers. Be careful with candles.

White with Accents of Color

Keep everything white. Use white table linens, white dishes and for the napkin, roll up and tie with white satin ribbon and include a sprig of rosemary. The color accents will come from the crystal bowl of the strawberry centerpieces.

Ice Sculpture

Ice sculptures would certainly be beautiful amidst evening candlelight. If your wedding is in the snow, have the ice sculpture outside with lights shining on it to make it sparkle. Many caterers can arrange this.

Speech Notes

If your best man is writing his speech, ask him for the actual written card and notes of the speech to include in your wedding scrapbook.

Your Parent's Wedding Photo

Make color copies or reprints of various photos and include them next to the wedding cake-- all in nice frames. Include your parents' wedding photo, your grandparent's wedding photo, and a picture of you and the groom as children.

Don't Look Now

Have candid photos taken at the reception. These photos are very appealing and give a glimpse into the real fun and entertainment.

Photos Documentary Style

Have your photographer take photos, documentary style. Ask them if they can use infrared film, as this will give your photos a very enchanting magical feel.

Beta Fighting Fish

For a bit of elegance, place tall vases with Calla Lilies, each with a Beta fighting fish in water.

Pumpkins

Arrange white tulle with sprinkled glitter and white candles in hurricane lamps, and include small pumpkins throughout the environment.

The Sky is the Limit

If the location permits, leave the church in a hot air balloon and head for the clouds.

Cinderella Effect

Place glass slippers on the tables with white twinkle lights and fresh daisies to give a fairytale Cinderella look to the whole affair.

Instant Camera

At each table have a black scrapbook and instant Camera with silver and gold milky pens and double sided tape. Ask guests to take some candid pictures and tape them in the scrapbook with a little message. You can only imagine the fun.

Wine Tasting Reception

Do you like wine? If so, why not have a wine tasting reception. Maybe you could have a local winery, restaurant or distributor sponsor the event.

Fabric-Look Cake

Order a white cake that is draped to look like fabric to match the bride's dress.

Sheet Music

Instead of a guest book, get the sheet music of the couples' first dance song and black fountain pens. Ask the guests to sign the sheet music, after the ceremony and have it framed.

Black Page Scrapbook

For the guest book, use a black page scrap book and have silver and gold pens available for guests to sign.

Rustic Garden

Create centerpieces made from combining flowes, spanish moss and with moss-covered urns. You can get spanish moss at most nurseries. Note: You can get green moss to grow on even new pots by brushing with natural, unflavored yogurt & keeping in a cool, moist spot for a few days.

Strawberries and Cream

Have guests greeted at the reception with champagne and strawberries with cream. That'll start it off right.

Groom's Cake Smashing

When it's time to feed your beautiful new bride the first piece of cake, add a little humor by smashing it in your own face. Or instead of smashing cake, why not have a big kiss given on the side of the groom's face with red lipstick to mark that occasion.

Slide Show

If your reception is a buffet style, put together a slide show and play it so all your guests will be entertained while waiting their turn.

Survival Kit

If you have a lot of guests that are flying in for the wedding, provide them a "city survival kit". Include a map of the city, attractions in the area, list of your favorite restaurants, and entertainment ideas available during their stay.

Sugared Fresh Flowers

Have sugared fresh flowers on your cake to add sparkle.

Wedding Toss

Instead of the traditional "wedding toss", ask the DJ to play one of your favorite songs and ask only those couples who have been married for ten years plus to dance. Every few minutes have the DJ dismiss couples by counting additional years until you have the longest married couple left dancing. This will be the couple to whom the bride happily gives her bouquet.

Piped in Music

Have Bagpipers play a traditional wedding song and pipe you into the reception and dinner hall.

Valentine's Day Cards

Use Valentine's Day cards for reception place cards.

Color Theme

Create a color theme for your wedding including invitations, flowers, wedding attire, reception decorating.

Special Story

Ask the DJ to announce that in order for the bride and groom to kiss, someone must stand and share a special story about them first. Be prepared, you might have to perform more than one kiss.

Skywriting

Have a skywriting plane write something special to the bride and groom.

Advice

Place a black journal with silver and gold and milky pens on each table. Attach a note to the front of the journal asking guests to write a favorite memory of the couple, or advice from their marriage to yours.

Dancing on a Cloud

For a really magical and enchanting event, when it's time for the first dance, arrange dry ice to cover the dance floor. This will give an enchanting effect of dancing on a cloud up in the air.

Flat Wine takes on a New Meaning
Take the first bottle of champagne at your reception as husband and wife and have it flattened and turned into something you will cherish forever: www.flatwine.com.

Freeze Dried Bouquet
Have your bouquet freeze dried, so you will remember it always.

Surprise Gift
On your bouquet, tie a small gift in a sachet for a surprise for the guest who catches the bouquet.

Musical Noisemakers
Place tiny musical noisemakers on the table, such as kazoos, trumpets, bells, horns and harmonicas on each table. Ask the DJ to announce to guests that if they want the bride and groom to kiss, they must play "*Here Comes the Bride*" with one of the noisemakers.

Twinkle Lights
Place lots of twinkle lights around the reception area to create a magical ambience!

Airplane Banner
Have an airplane banner flown over your reception site at a specific time to congratulate the new couple.

Goldfish Bowl

As centerpieces, have a goldfish bowl with 2 fancy goldfish. Tape a bag of fish food under one of the chairs and the guest that has the chair with the fish food gets to take home the fish.

Reception Lighting

Keep the lighting at a dim level. Remember too, everyone looks great by the glow of candlelight.

Balloons Traveled

After the reception have helium balloons released with a message inside including your names, wedding date, location, and include an e-mail address for the person who finds the balloon to e-mail the couple so as to track how far the balloons traveled.

Romantic Arbor

If you're planning an outdoor wedding and want a romantic arbor, look for one in your favorite garden store and decorate with ivy and flowers. After the ceremony you can use it in your own backyard.

Sunflowers

Use sunflowers as centerpieces. Get a tall vase and include the tall and dramatic sunflowers that look like they are smiling back at you.

Mini Christmas Trees

Set up mini Christmas trees tied at the base with beautiful satin ribbon as centerpieces for a winter wedding.

Party Hats

Create a fun environment with lots of confetti, sound makers, balloons and party hats.

Donate Flower Centerpieces

When your magical evening has come to an end, and you're trying to decide what to do with the centerpieces, why not donate them to the Children's Hospital?

Rose Petal Farewell

As the bride and groom are departing the reception, have rose petals sprinkled on them for good luck.

Kid's Area

Set up an area especially for your younger guests. Include meals for kids like mini pizzas, hamburgers, grilled cheese, etc.

Time for the Bubbly

When it's time to open the bubbly, have the bride and groom pop the cork and walk around to pour each guest's glass. This is a good way for the couple to say a quick hello to guests, as well as pouring their champagne.

Tiny Flower Ice Cubes

Freeze tiny fresh edible flowers inside the ice cube trays for a delicate, cool effect in the refreshments.

Future Memories

Have a black-and-white picture of the bride and groom blown up, with a black matte border around the picture. Have the guests use a gold or silver pen to sign the picture border.

The Announcements

Have the bride and groom announce their wedding party instead of the DJ, including how long they've known each other, and a toast to one another.

Sparklers
As a magical effect at the end of the evening, give your guests sparklers to light as you depart the reception on your way to live happily ever after.

Monte Carlo Casino Reception

Get your guests trying their luck at the tables by playing Black Jack, Craps and Poker. This will be a crowd pleaser with guests wanting to linger.

Portraits
Hire a couple of artists to set up easels and do quick portraits of your guests.

Giant Carmel Apples

SUNGLASSES

Personalized Snow Globes

Lottery Tickets

MAGICAL

Favors

Weddings are one of the few events where guests are fed, entertained, and then given a parting gift. What small gift will you give your guests as a reminder of the wedding event? Chocolates wrapped in beautiful tulle make a simple, but elegant gift. For those of you working with bigger budgets, bottles of wine or expensive cigars make appropriate gifts. This section includes a number of magical favor ideas for every type of occasion and every budget.

Irresistable Chocolate

Give Chocolate wedding favors dressed in ribbons that match your color scheme.

Swiss Army Knives

If the wedding is not too big, give a practical gift such as a miniature key chain style Swiss Army Knife with your new name and wedding date engraved on it. Your local promotional items company can accommodate you.

Give the Gift of Music for Your Gifts

www.cdnow.com will put together a custom CD for your special day.

Magical Promotional Items

Matchbooks with imprinted names of the couple; candy bars, lollipops with romantic sayings imprinted on the sticks, miniature vases with flowers, potted plants, snow globes, magnets, lollipops, sunglasses, imprinted coffee cups filled with flowers, wine glasses, champagne glasses etched with the couples names, golf balls or golf tees, tennis balls, baseball caps, imprinted t-shirts, framed engagement photo of the couple, imprinted frisbees.

Luck of the Numbers

A Lottery ticket in an envelope with a photo of the couple is always a nice touch.

Tiny Petit Fours
The perfect French touch to an edible favor.

Have a Cigar
A chocolate cigar with a band imprinted with the couples' name and wedding date.

The Real Cigar and Brandy
How about giving your guests a real cigar and miniature bottle of brandy tied together with a bow and a note that says "Enjoy life's little pleasures, like we found ours."

Wake Up and Smell the Coffee Beans
Keep your guests going with chocolate coffee cordials... chocolate covered espresso beans you can purchase at your favorite coffee house.

Personalized Coasters
Have personalized coasters of your wedding day, beautiful enough that your guests will cherish. 4 pack per guest.

Beautiful Ornaments
For a Winter wedding, buy some beautiful ornaments and write your names and wedding date on them for everyone to take home.

Snow Globes
Include a magical winter snow globe for your guest.

Personalize Your Wine Bottles
For your Reception with a special message, www.wine.com will have you select the wine you'd like, then you can customize a pre-made label or even design your own original.

Ooh La La! Small Bottle of French Wine
Give your guests a small bottle of French wine with your own label designed from www.wine.com.

Gourmet Lollipop,Lollipops!
Go to your favorite local candy store and select from the many colors and gourmet flavors and tie them up with a beautiful satin ribbon.

Plastic Sunglasses
Have the wedding couple's name and date printed on the frames. Look in your local phone book or check websites for promotional items. Have the photographer get a group shot of everyone wearing their sunglasses.

Keepsake Sound Makers
Include bride and groom's name and wedding date.

Golf Tees

For the golf enthusiasts, golf tees with bride and groom's name and wedding date as a favor.

Miniature Baskets with a Selection of Potpourri

Include sachets of potpourri in lace, French chocolates, a miniature bottle of wine, cheese and crackers, tea, chocolate French coffee cordials, flower seed packets symbolizing growth and future with the wedding date and couple's name, mints, etc.

White Roses

Use a simple long stem white rose placed across everyone's plate as a memento of the day along with a thank you card.

Personalized CD

Create a personalized CD and make a CD label with the bride and groom's name, as well as, wedding date and personalized message

Seed Packets

As a favor, print up little notes saying something about plant these seeds and watch them grow as a reminder of our wedding day.

Small Vases

From a floral supply or craft store, inscribe the bride and groom's wedding information and place at each setting with a single flower. Encourage guests to take them as favors.

Autumn Weddings

Place decorated caramel apples as favors for your guest to enjoy toward the end of the evening.

Penny for your Thoughts

If your reception site has a fountain, place a penny at each guest's seat with a note to make a wish at the fountain.

Gourmet Brides and Grooms

From the gourmet minded couple, write some of your favorite recipes along with your names and wedding date on a creative recipe card. Place one on each guest's plate as a favor.

FAMOUS CHOCOLATE, CHOCOLATE CHIP COOKIES

1 1/4 cups all-purpose flour
2 tablespoons unsweetened Dutch-process cocoa powder
1 teaspoon baking powder
3/4 teaspoon salt
1 pound fine-quality bittersweet chocolate (not unsweetened)
1 stick (1/2 cup) unsalted butter
1/2 cup sugar
3 large eggs

Preheat oven to 350°F. and line a large baking sheet with parchment paper.
Into a bowl sift together flour, cocoa and baking powders, and salt. Coarsely chop chocolate. In a double boiler or a large metal bowl set over a saucepan of barely simmering water melt butter with three fourths chocolate, stirring until smooth.
Remove chocolate mixture from heat and stir in sugar. Stir in eggs 1 at a time until combined well and stir in flour mixture until just combined. Chill dough, covered, at least 10 minutes and up to 1 hour. Drop rounded tablespoon measures of dough about 1, inches apart onto baking sheet and stud each cookie with a few pieces remaining chocolate. Bake in middle of oven 10 minutes, or until just set. Cool cookies on sheet on rack 5 minutes and transfer with a spatula to rack to cool completely. Make more cookies with remaining dough in same manner.
Makes about 36 cookies.

No Family Stress

Cost Effective

Destination Weddings

Do Exactly What You Want

MAGICAL Eloping & Destination Weddings

Every year more American couples - swayed by the allure and romance of foreign locales - are opting for destination weddings. Couples traveling to foreign countries can choose to incorporate local marriage customs and ambiance into their marriage ceremonies. There are an unlimited number of romantic venues available throughout the world, offering spectacular accommodations, amazing restaurants, and magical surroundings. If you know where to look, romantic castles and fantasy settings can be part of your wedding reality.

Times Have Changed
Years ago, getting married away from home meant you were eloping, which carried a stigma ranging from scandalous, mysterious, and adventurous to romantic. Couples would venture out on their own terms, traveling away from disapproving families and wed at outside locations generally within the United States. Things have changed for the better, it is no longer consider scandalous to elope.

Cost Effective
Eloping is generally far less expensive than a medium to large wedding. Combining your wedding with your honeymoon has definite economic advantages. This is especially true in countries where the dollar is usually strong. Whether it's a lavish ceremony or an intimate vow exchange atop a mountain in Colorado, you get to customize the special event to your tastes and budget.

Eliminate Family Stress
Destination weddings allow you to take out the family stress factor so you can keep it simple and enjoy the experience. It becomes your unique occasion rather than someone else's idea of what they would like. This is a time when you get to call the shots and make up all the rules. Create your own idea of a magical wedding, or vow renewal, the way you've always wished it to be.

Exciting Europe Before, During and After the Ceremony

Whatever your background and interests, eloping has something for everybody. While tying the knot, why not consider Europe? There's plenty to experience before, during and after your ceremony. Imagine wine tasting in a Tuscan Italian village, take a helicopter ride across the Scottish lochs and glens, or take a cooking class at the famed Cordon Blue Cooking School in Paris. Some wedding planners can even arrange for you to meet the Pope in the Vatican City. It's really up to your imagination and interests to create your custom magical wedding.

Elope to Europe

Eloping Locations and Websites

Martha's Vineyard
www.mvol.com

Maine
www.maineweddings.com

Grand Canyon
www.gcanyon.com

Niagara Falls
www.occasionsniagara.com

Lake Tahoe
www.weddingstahoe.com

Napa Valley
www.napavalley.com

Yosemite National Park
www.mariposa.yosemite.net

Sedona, Arizona
www.sedonaweddings.com

Magical Locations

Destination Wedding & Eloping

Big Hollywood Production

Take the Kids!

Marry in a Castle

Small

Intimate

Wedding

Vow Renewals & Second Weddings

Renewing your wedding vows? Planning a second-plus wedding? There are so many possibilities open to you, from the warmth and simplicity of a summer backyard wedding to a wedding and reception staged against the backdrop of the French countryside. Children also bring charming and loving new elements to wedding ceremonies. Nowadays, it's not uncommon for children to participate in every stage of the wedding process, as well as accompany their parents on the honeymoon. Read the following suggestions, and then use the wisdom and self-knowledge you've acquired to design the magical "first" wedding you've always wanted.

You're Invited
for a Vow Renewal in the
Hills of Tuscany, Italy

Where the Magic Began

Go back to where the magic began and get married where you first met.

Take the Kids

Take the kids with you and relive the day and location where you first married.

Pick Anywhere in the World

Since there are no legal requirements needed to renew your vows, the world is yours. Renewing your vows can be done anywhere, such as at a house, at your favorite beach, park, a castle in Europe, a winery, a place of worship, restaurant or any special place you like. You don't need the clergy to make it legal, so you can be as creative as you wish.

Marry in a castle

Get married in Scotland like Madonna.

Hills of Tuscany

Go to the hills of Tuscany and then attend a local cooking school.

Cannes Film Festival

Re-new your vows in Cannes during the film festival, you're sure to see some celebrities.

Display your Original Wedding Album

Don't forget the original wedding album to show to new guests and to remember the good times.

Original Wedding Dress

Wear your original wedding dress, cocktail dress, a formal gown, suit or whatever seems appropriate for the location and theme.

Groom's Original Attire

The groom could wear the original tuxedo, suit or whatever seems right for the occasion. Write your vows to reflect how you've enjoyed the time together. Reading the vows; Have your children or friends do the readings of your vows.

Begin Your Own Tradition

If your parents or grandparents didn't marry locally, why not begin your own tradition and marry in a new venue that can be passed down. Select a special place that can be a venue for generations to come. Encourage your kids or grandkids to marry where you did. Be creative and enjoy the opportunity.

Have a Big "Hollywood Production" Wedding

It doesn't have to be for first ceremonies only.

Updated Wedding Vows

Renew your vows to your spouse in an updated version that reflects your current lifestyle. Include your children and grandchildren. Relive the past while including the present for future memories. It's fun for not only the couple, but for other family members and friends as well.

Wear Your Original Wedding Dress

Keep your vow renewal celebration simple or make it an all out bash with friends, family and business associates.

Here's how the invite might read:

We request the honor of your presence
for the renewal
of the wedding vows of
Mr. and Mrs. (couples name)

Here's another version

We, the children (and grandchildren)
of Mr. and Mrs. (couples name)
duly request the honor of your presence
for the vow renewal ceremony
for our parents (grandparents)

Second Weddings
Stress Free. Plan a honeymoon and second wedding all in one, without all of the family stress.

Take a Chance
Pick a location and theme you would have never selected the first time around.

Charitable Gifts
Do you have everything you need from your first wedding? How about asking your guests to make a charitable contribution to your favorite charity or cause, instead of traditional gifts.

Register at a Travel Agency
Inform your guests that you're registered at a travel agency and monies are going towards your honeymoon fund or destination wedding.

See the Location sections for some magical ideas that you may not have done the first time around.

His and Her Spa

African Safari

Cordon Bleu Cooking Class

Shakesphere's Homeland

CHAMPAGNE COUNTRY, FRANCE

MAGICAL Honeymoons

The big day is behind you now, and who more than you deserve rest and relaxation? If you're a couple who thrives on fast paced activities, then select a dynamic honeymoon location that provides you with lots of stimulation. If you prefer escaping the masses, choose a secluded spot to enjoy and explore your new relationship. No rules to follow here, just take it all in and smile. There are an unlimited number of destinations to choose, each offering it's own special appeal. Plan ahead, keeping your budget in mind, and remember to document the occasion with photos and video.

Personal Postcards

During your honeymoon, send each other a personal postcard home each day saying what you did that day together or what a wonderful time you're having, etc. Keep a secret what you write, and when you return home you will have several personal postcards awaiting you. You can also put together a postcard journal with the entire collection.

Honeymoon Packages

When booking your honeymoon, ask the hotel if they have "honeymoon packages". Some hotels do everything from put champagne in your room, to a room upgrade, to rose petals sprinkled in your room.

All-Inclusive Resorts

Pay all upfront and then begin the honeymoon without having to worry about paying for a thing.

His and Her Spa

Now that the stress of the wedding day is over, choose from one of the many locations with a spa and pamper yourselves.

Try Something New

Wherever you go, try a helicopter ride or hot air balloon. Feel as free as the birds.

Outdoors People

Include snorkeling, hiking, biking, skiing, surfing, sailing, water skiing, wind surfing or fishing, to complete your outdoors active honeymoon.

Cruise Through your Honeymoon

Select from one of many cruise ships that sail through the Caribbean, Alaska or Mexico.

Pick a Location Where our US Dollar is Strong

How about South Africa? Our dollar is very strong and you can go diamond mining, wine tasting, and end with a safari. South Africa has it all.

African Safari

Join the African wildlife and camp amongst them under the African sky. See the Internet for South Africa and Kenya's various safari packages.

For Those Gourmet Cooks

Select a location that offers a gourmet cooking class. You can select from Cordon Bleu France, England or Canada-- or a Tuscan cooking school in Italy.

Favorite U.S. Honeymoon Locations

You don't have to go farther than your own backyard to find a great honeymoon spot here in the good old USA.

The San Francisco Treat

There's lots of cosmopolitan style here, with plenty of things to do. Take a cable car ride through the city or visit:

Alcatraz
Fisherman's Wharf
Great restaurants
Theater
Shopping

We love L.A.

Experience Los Angeles and live like the stars do. Enjoy the glitzy area of Beverly Hills to the trendy Melrose Avenue... and don't forget Venice Beach.

Great museums and galleries
Restaurants
Santa Monica Pier
Disneyland, Knott's Berry Farm, Universal Studios, and Magic Mountain
Get tickets to be in the audience of a game show or sitcom.
Wonderful coastline

San Diego, the Best Kept Secret
Sea World
World famous San Diego Zoo
Spectacular beaches and bays
Balboa Park
La Jolla
Seaport Village
Coronado Island
Hotel del Coronado

Florida
Disney World
Epcott Center
Florida Keys
South Beach

Aloha, Hawaiian Style
This is America's favorite honeymoon spot. Can you blame us? Tropical beaches and balmy breezes, for all the sun worshipers.

Go to a Luau and feel like a real Hawaiian with hula dancing.

Take a helicopter ride for a tropical experience from the sky.

Island hopping. Visit the many faces of Hawaii by visiting the other islands.

Bicycle down a volcano bike path followed by mimosas at sunrise or sunset.

Snorkel with the Pacific's beautifully colored fish.

Fly to Europe

Begin your new lives feeling like a Prince and Princess by flying off to Europe. Plan out your itinerary in one, or several countries. If you haven't been to Europe and want to start off easy, fly into London so you can start off in an English speaking country and work your way from there.

France

Visit Monet's water gardens in France. West of Paris see the beautiful water gardens at Claude Monet's home. You'll be able to stroll the garden, as well as, tour the house.

Sample Champagne tasting in the real Champagne Country North of Paris. An easy train ride as this is the official home of champagne. Just like wine tasting, you are able to explore the caves and sample real French champagne.

For Gourmet Cooks

Select a location that also offers a gourmet cooking class all in one. Think the Cordon Bleu in Paris. Reserve a date for a demonstration class, or an entire week.

Rent a Car and Expolore the Countryside

Rent a car, and visit the Loire Valley and do some

wine tasting. Drive through the South of France and look for celebrities during the Cannes Film Festival.

Italy

Visit a Tuscan cooking school. Turn your honey-moon into a culinary delight in one of the beautiful Tuscany cooking schools.

Take a Roman holiday. Explore all the roman ruins, as well as, see some of the best artwork in the world. Indulge yourself, because this will be some of the best food you will ever have. Try a Venetian experience. Visit where there's more water than land. Take a romantic gondola ride and let your new lives together begin in style.

Honeymoon Postcard

Split of Champagne

Thank You Note Party

MOVIE PASSES

MAGICAL

Thank You Notes

Say, "thank you" with magical style. You may receive many gifts ranging from toasters, to money to complete honeymoon packages. And no matter how small or large, each gift provides you with an opportunity to share your appreciation in a way that will never be forgotten. Something as simple as sending a friendly "hello" and "thank you" postcards from your honeymoon destination can be a creative and inexpensive way to show your gratitude. Read on for more ideas...

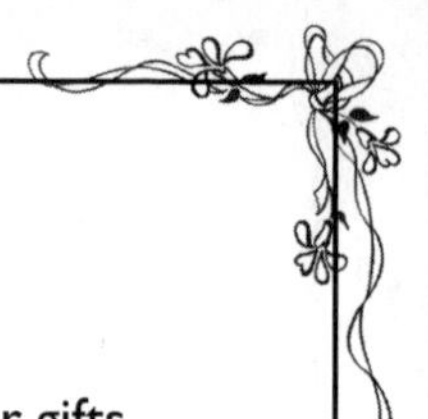

Make Life a Little Easier
Write each thank you note as you receive your gifts, or once a week, as this will keep you sane in the end. Everyday will feel magical as the UPS truck arrives daily.

Spending the Cash
If you receive the ultimate magical gift of money, make sure you include how you plan to spend it.

Thank You Note Party
Turn the thank you notes process into a little party. Get your new spouse to help. Create the mood by having your favorite snacks, a bottle of wine, and your favorite music as you write your notes together. Your messages will reflect how you feel while enjoying yourself as you write.

Capture the Moment
Have someone taking pictures of guests as they enter the reception. After the pictures are developed, have an extra copy made and include them with your "thank you" notes. Your guests will have a personal memory of your big day.

Personal Touch
Add a personal touch and hand write the addresses on your envelopes. Address them in calligraphy as an extra added touch.

Wallet Size Wedding Photo
Include a wallet size photo of your favorite wedding picture inside each thank you note.

Wedding Video
For guests who were unable to attend, but sent a gift, send them a copy of your wedding video.Attach a special thank you note so they will feel like they were there.

Split of Champagne
For guests who were also assisting with the wedding, include a split of champagne with a thank you note.

Lottery Ticket
Include a lottery ticket with the thank you note in hopes that your guest strikes it rich.

Bouquet of Flowers
If you only have a few thank you notes to send, say your thank you with flowers.

Digital Video
Send a personalized "thank you" video clip via e-mail for each guests that are able to receive e-mails.

Custom Thank You Notes
Design your own thank you notes using computer software and print out on you own desktop printer. Inexpensive and magically creative.

Movie Passes
For that extra special thank you, include 2 movie passes with a note thanking them for being a part of your "wedding movie production", now have some fun and enjoy the movie of your choice.

Include a Fun Rhyme of the Wedding Day
Sit down and really think about your wedding day. Create a little rhyme describing your wonderful wedding day event.

Dream House Fund
If you received money that you will be putting toward a house, include a picture of your dream house.

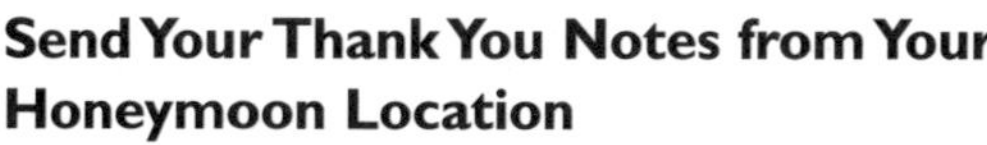

Send Your Thank You Notes from Your Honeymoon Location

How about taking your thank you notes with you on your honeymoon and have them postmarked and mailed from your honeymoon location. If you're going somewhere exotic, include a piece of memorabilia from that location.

Honeymoon Photo Thank You Card

Include a honeymoon photo along with your thank you note to include everyone in your travel experience.

Honeymoon Postcards
Send a postcard from your honeymoon as your "thank you" and they will know exactly where you traveled.

Greetings from Paris!

Hello from Paris!
Thank you for the gift certificate that helped us get to Paris.
We're having the time of our lives!
Best wishes...
Ted & Suzanne

Electronic Thank You Cards
Send an electronic thank you postcard from www.bluemountain.com in addition to the regular cards.

Tagline

Include the words "Thank you for being part of our Fairytale"

Congratulations!

HAVE A CUP OF COFFEE

Enjoy your day!

Take a Break

Relax

Conclusion

The Time of Our Lives

It's a wonderful time to get married, because of the wide variety of creative options available to couples these days. Weddings today range from big expensive Hollywood-style weddings, to theme weddings. From simple but elegant weddings, to destination weddings. They're all equally accepted in today's society. They're customized to fit the style and budget of the betrothing couple and reflect the diversity of today's culture. Although, there is one common element between them--they all have the potential of becoming overwhelming. So, you can appreciate the value of wedding coordinators and brides planning their own weddings. I hope my book will give you a few creative ideas that will help launch your own magical wedding experience. After the wedding, your performance of a lifetime will actually be over. So, remember to take a bow, because all that planning and celebration will have finally come to a wonderful conclusion. And, if through all the festivity, your efforts appear underappreciated, I'd like to say in advance, *you've done a great job creating your magical wedding*. You will deserve that relaxing honeymoon. So afterward, sit back, stretch out and enjoy that special person for whom the entire ceremony was performed.

It has been my pleasure to share some creative ideas with you from my experience and knowledge. I know your wedding will be a magical success, along with your future life together. Keep the magic alive and congratulations!

creative feedback

www.magicwandweddings.com

Tell me What you Think

Write to me...

Do you have comments and ideas you'd like to share with me and others? I'd love to hear about the fun, magical ideas you incorporated into your wedding. Thank you in advance for your help.

Please e-mail me at: info@magicwandweddings.com

Visit my Website at

www.magicwandweddings.com

I've included many creative services and products to help you create your own magical wedding.

Unique Ideas
Travel
Go Shopping/Bridal Jewelry
Wedding Supplies
Free Samples
Invitations & Favors
Recipes and more!

We are continuously adding new creative services and products to the MagicWand website, to provide you with up-to-date unique information in the wedding industry, so visit us often.

Notes

Notes

MAGIC
WAND
PUBLISHING